CW00346974

Couscous

A Delicious Couscous Cookbook Filled
with Easy Couscous Recipes

By
BookSumo Press
All rights reserved

Published by
http://www.booksumo.com

LEGAL NOTES

All Rights Reserved. No Part Of This Book May Be Reproduced Or Transmitted In Any Form Or By Any Means. Photocopying, Posting Online, And / Or Digital Copying Is Strictly Prohibited Unless Written Permission Is Granted By The Book's Publishing Company. Limited Use Of The Book's Text Is Permitted For Use In Reviews Written For The Public.

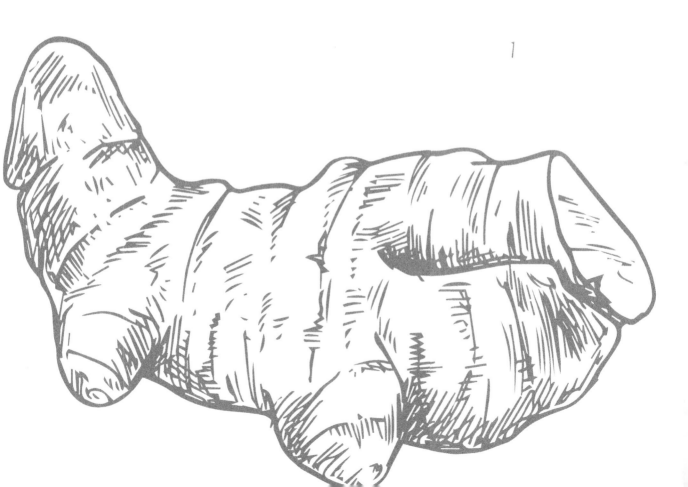

Parmesan Pecan Couscous

Prep Time: 30 mins
Total Time: 35 mins

Servings per Recipe: 7
Calories	316.7
Fat	13.4 g
Cholesterol	9.4 mg
Sodium	392.1 mg
Carbohydrates	36.8 g
Protein	12.9 g

Ingredients

1 medium onion, chopped
2 garlic cloves, minced
2 tbsp. olive oil
1 (14 1/2 oz.) cans chicken broth
1 (10 oz.) packages frozen chopped spinach
1 (10 oz.) packages couscous

3/4 C. fresh grated parmesan cheese
2 tbsp. lemon juice
salt
fresh ground pepper
1/2 C. chopped pecans, toasted

Directions

1. Place a large saucepan over medium heat. Heat in it the oil.
2. Cook in it the onion with garlic for 3 min. Stir in the spinach with broth.
3. Cook them for 3 min while stirring often. Cook them until they start boiling.
4. Stir in the couscous and put on the lid. Let them sit for 6 min.
5. Once the time is up, stir in the remaining ingredients and fluff them with a fork.
6. Serve your couscous salad right away.
7. Enjoy.

SARANAC
Lakehouse
Couscous

Prep Time: 10 mins
Total Time: 20 mins

Servings per Recipe: 8
Calories	148.3
Fat	1.4 g
Cholesterol	0.0 mg
Sodium	7.6 mg
Carbohydrates	28.5 g
Protein	4.7 g

Ingredients

2 C. nonfat vegetable broth
1 tsp. dried basil
1 tsp. minced garlic
1 1/2 C. uncooked couscous
3 tbsp. balsamic vinegar
2 tsp. olive oil

1/4 tsp. ground pepper
5 small tomatoes, peeled and chopped

Directions

1. Place a large saucepan over medium heat. Heat in it the broth until it starts boiling.
2. Add the basil with garlic. Stir in the couscous and put on the lid.
3. Turn off the lid and let it sit for 8 min.
4. Get a mixing bowl: Mix in it the balsamic vinegar, the oil, and the pepper.
5. Add the mixture to the couscous with tomato, and vinegar dressing.
6. Stir them to coat. Serve your salad right away.
7. Enjoy.

Couscous
Salad I
(Southwest Style)

🥣 Prep Time: 10 mins
🕐 Total Time: 15 mins

Servings per Recipe: 10
Calories   226.6
Fat   5.0 g
Cholesterol   0.0 mg
Sodium   99.9 mg
Carbohydrates   37.3 g
Protein   9.6 g

Ingredients

1 C. uncooked couscous
1 1/4 C. chicken broth
3 tbsp. extra virgin olive oil
2 tbsp. fresh lime juice
1 tsp. apple cider vinegar
1/2 tsp. ground cumin
8 green onions, chopped

1 red bell pepper, seeded and chopped
1/4 C. chopped fresh cilantro
1 C. frozen corn kernels, thawed
2 (15 oz.) cans black beans, drained
salt and pepper

Directions

1. Place a large saucepan over medium heat. Heat in it the broth until it starts boiling.
2. Add the couscous and stir it well. Put on the lid and turn off the heat.
3. Let it sit for 6 min.
4. Get a mixing bowl: Mix in it the olive oil, lime juice, vinegar, and cumin.
5. Stir in the green onions, red pepper, cilantro, corn, and beans.
6. Stir the rice with a fork then add it to the bowl and toss them to coat.
7. Adjust the seasoning of your salad. Place it in the fridge and let it sit until ready to serve.
8. Enjoy.

COUSCOUS
Salad II
(Almond and
Berries)

Prep Time: 20 mins
Total Time: 25 mins

Servings per Recipe: 6
Calories	235.6
Fat	12.2 g
Cholesterol	0.0 mg
Sodium	191.4 mg
Carbohydrates	25.6 g
Protein	6.2 g

Ingredients
1 1/2 C. chicken broth
1/2 C. dried cranberries
1 tsp.. ground cinnamon
1/4 tsp.. ground cumin
1 C. uncooked couscous
1/4-1/3 C. vegetable oil
2 tbsp. rice vinegar

1/3-1/2 C. sliced almonds, toasted
1/3 C. chopped green onion
2 tbsp. chopped of fresh mint

Directions
1. Place a pot over medium heat. Stir in it the broth, cranberries, cinnamon, and cumin.
2. Cook them until they start boiling. Turn off the heat and add the couscous.
3. Put on the lid and let them sit for 6 min.
4. Once the time is up, stir them with a fork. Let them sit for a few more minutes to cool down.
5. Get a mixing bowl: Mix in it the oil with vinegar. Add them to the couscous with the rest of the ingredients.
6. Stir them to coat. Serve your couscous immediately or chill it in the fridge until ready to serve.
7. Enjoy.

Cardamom
Currants Couscous

Prep Time: 15 mins
Total Time: 27 mins

Servings per Recipe: 4
Calories   546.2
Fat   23.3 g
Cholesterol   49.8 mg
Sodium   698.6 mg
Carbohydrates   71.4 g
Protein   13.9 g

Ingredients

1/4 C. butter
1/4 tsp. cinnamon, ground
1/4 tsp. cardamom, ground
1/8 tsp. clove, ground
2 1/4 C. chicken stock
1/2 C. currants
1 1/2 C. couscous

2 tbsp. butter
1/2 tsp. salt
1/4 C. cashews, toasted and chopped

Directions

1. Place a saucepan over low heat. Heat in it 1/4 C. of butter until it melts.
2. Stir in the cinnamon with cardamom, and clove. Cook them for 1 to 2 min while stirring.
3. Stir in the currants with stock. Cook them until they start boiling.
4. Stir in the couscous with 2 tbsp. of butter.
5. Turn off the heat and put on the lid. Let them sit for 6 min.
6. Stir your couscous well with a fork. Adjust its seasoning then serve it with some toasted nuts.
7. Enjoy.

ITALIAN
Herbed with Beans

 Prep Time: 5 mins
Total Time: 10 mins

Servings per Recipe: 4
Calories	448.5
Fat	21.1 g
Cholesterol	33.3 mg
Sodium	592.8 mg
Carbohydrates	49.9 g
Protein	16.1 g

Ingredients

1 C. couscous
2 tbsp. lemon juice
2 tbsp. olive oil
1/3 C. green onion
2 medium tomatoes, diced
1 C. canned red kidney beans

1 C. feta cheese
1/4 C. pine nuts
2 tbsp. oregano

Directions

1. Get a bowl: Stir in it the couscous with 1 C. of boiling water.
2. Put on the lid and let it sit for 5 to 6 min. Fluff it with a fork.
3. Get a mixing bowl: Mix in it the lemon juice and olive oil.
4. Add it to the couscous with a pinch of salt and pepper.
5. Mix them well serve it.
6. Enjoy.

Plum Tomato and Olive Couscous with Peas

Prep Time: 10 mins
Total Time: 10 mins

Servings per Recipe: 4
Calories   453.0
Fat   14.7 g
Cholesterol   16.6 mg
Sodium   938.5 mg
Carbohydrates   64.7 g
Protein   16.1 g

Ingredients

1 1/2 C. chicken broth
1 C. uncooked couscous
1/2-1 tsp. dried oregano
2 plum tomatoes, chopped
1 - 2 C. diced peeled cucumber
1/2 C. crumbled feta cheese
1/2 C. small ripe olives, halved
1 small red onion, finely chopped

1 (15 oz.) cans chickpeas, well drained
1/4 C. water
3 tbsp. lemon juice
2 - 3 tbsp. olive oil
1 tsp. fresh ground black pepper
salt

Directions

1. Place a pot over medium heat. Heat in it 1 1/2 C. of broth until they start boiling.
2. Add the couscous with oregano. Put on the lid and turn off the heat.
3. Let them sit for 5 to 6 min. Add the tomatoes with cucumber, olives, feta, chickpeas, and onion.
4. Mix them well and place them aside.
5. Get a mixing bowl: Whisk in it 1/4 C. of water with lemon juice, olive oil, a pinch of salt and pepper.
6. Add it to the couscous and mix them well. Serve it right away.
7. Enjoy.

GINGER
Pepper Couscous

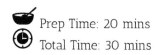 Prep Time: 20 mins

Total Time: 30 mins

Servings per Recipe: 4
Calories   275.9
Fat   2.1 g
Cholesterol   0.0 mg
Sodium   342.5 mg
Carbohydrates   54.3 g
Protein   10.3 g

Ingredients

1/2 tsp. vegetable oil
2 green onions, chopped
1 sweet red pepper
1 garlic clove, minced
2 tomatoes, chopped
1 zucchini, diced
1 C. chickpeas, cooked
1 C. boiling water
1/4 tsp. salt

1/2 tsp. curry powder
1 tsp. ground cumin
2 tbsp. fresh parsley
1/8 tsp. ground cinnamon
1/2 tsp. ginger
1/4 tsp. cayenne
1 C. couscous

Directions

1. Place a large pan over medium heat. Heat in it the oil.
2. Cook in it the green onions, sweet pepper, garlic, tomatoes and zucchini for 6 min while stirring often.
3. Turn off the heat and place it aside.
4. Place a pot over medium heat. Stir in the remaining ingredients.
5. Put on the lid and let them sit for 6 min. Mix them well with a fork.
6. Serve your warm couscous with the veggies salsa.
7. Enjoy.

Couscous
Salad IV (Cucumber and Tomatoes)

Prep Time: 20 mins
Total Time: 30 mins

Servings per Recipe: 6
Calories   206.2
Fat   3.5 g
Cholesterol   0.0 mg
Sodium   63.3 mg
Carbohydrates   37.2 g
Protein   6.4 g

Ingredients

1 (8 7/8 oz.) packages Israeli couscous
1/2 medium cucumber, peeled and diced
2 medium tomatoes, seeded and chopped
1/4 C. red bell pepper, diced
2 - 3 green onions, sliced
10 black olives, sliced
6 oz. fat-free feta cheese, crumbled

2 tbsp. fresh tarragon, chopped fine
1 tsp. dried oregano
1 tbsp. fresh parsley, chopped fine
2 tbsp. lemon juice
1 tbsp. apple cider vinegar
1 tbsp. olive oil

Directions

1. Prepare the couscous by following the instructions on the package.
2. Add to it the rest of the ingredients. Mix them well then put on the lid.
3. Let it sit in the fridge for at least 15 min then serve it.
4. Enjoy.

WINTER
Carnival
Couscous

Prep Time: 20 mins
Total Time: 1 hr 20 mins

Servings per Recipe: 8
Calories   144.4
Fat   1.3 g
Cholesterol   0.0 mg
Sodium   32.1 mg
Carbohydrates   26.2 g
Protein   8.0 g

Ingredients

1 large onion, chopped
1 stalk celery, chopped
1 tsp. olive oil
4 medium carrots, grated
2 medium zucchini, grated
1 C. red lentil, rinsed and drained
6 C. vegetable broth

1 tsp. salt, to taste
1/2 tsp. ground pepper
1/2 tsp. dried basil
1/3 C. couscous

Directions

1. Place a pot over medium heat. Heat in it the oil.
2. Cook in it the celery with onion for 6 min. Stir in 1 tbsp. of water and cook them for 1 min.
3. Stir in the carrot with zucchini, lentils, broth, salt, basil, and pepper.
4. Turn the heat to high and cook them until they start boiling.
5. Lower the heat and put on half a cover. Cook them for 46 min while stirring often.
6. Stir in the couscous and cook them for 9 to 10 min.
7. Once the time is up, adjust the seasoning of your soup then serve it hot.
8. Enjoy.

Easy
Veggie Couscous

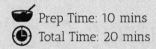 Prep Time: 10 mins
🕐 Total Time: 20 mins

Servings per Recipe: 4
Calories	168.7
Fat	4.1 g
Cholesterol	0.0 mg
Sodium	18.8 mg
Carbohydrates	27.8 g
Protein	5.8 g

Ingredients
1 1/2 lbs. zucchini, cut into 1/4 inch cubes
1 tbsp. olive oil
1/2 tsp. ground cumin

1 C. boiling water
2/3 C. couscous

Directions
1. Place a large pan over medium heat. Heat in it the oil.
2. Cook in it the zucchini with cumin, salt, and pepper.
3. Cook them for 6 min. Stir in the water and cook them until they start boiling.
4. Turn off the heat and add the couscous. Put on the lid and let them sit for 6 min.
5. Use a fork to mix them well then serve your couscous warm.
6. Enjoy.

SUMMER
Citrus Couscous

Prep Time: 10 mins
Total Time: 15 mins

Servings per Recipe: 4
Calories   129.2
Fat   0.2 g
Cholesterol   0.0 mg
Sodium   153.0 mg
Carbohydrates   26.8 g
Protein   4.3 g

Ingredients
1 1/4 C. water
3/4 C. uncooked couscous
1/4 C. sliced green onion
2 tbsp. finely chopped fresh parsley
2 tbsp. orange juice
1 tsp. grated lemon rind
1 tbsp. fresh lemon juice

1/4 tsp. salt
1/8 tsp. black pepper

Directions
1. Place a large saucepan over high heat. Heat in it the water until it starts boiling.
2. Add the couscous. Put on the lid and turn off the heat. Let them sit for 6 min.
3. Mix them with a fork. Add the orange juice with onion, parsley, lemon rind and juice, salt and pepper.
4. Mix them well then serve it with some chopped nuts.
5. Enjoy.

Rachel's
COUSCOUS

Prep Time: 15 mins
Total Time: 15 mins

Servings per Recipe: 4
Calories	609.7
Fat	11.9 g
Cholesterol	42.4 mg
Sodium	738.9 mg
Carbohydrates	83.6 g
Protein	40.4 g

Ingredients

2 C. instant couscous
2 C. boiling chicken stock
1 1/2 tsp. curry powder
1 1/2 tsp. garlic, minced
1 tbsp. margarine
13 oz. cans tuna in water, flaked & drained
1 red capsicum, diced

1 large carrot, grated
1.5 oz. baby rocket, or arugula
4 spring onions, thinly sliced
2 tbsp. lemon juice
2/3 C. hummus, to serve

Directions

1. Get a mixing bowl: Mix in it the stock with curry powder, and garlic.
2. Stir in the couscous and put on the lid. Let them sit for 6 min.
3. Mix them with a fork then add the tuna with capsicum, carrot, rocket, onions, lemon juice, a pinch of salt and pepper.
4. Serve your couscous with some hummus.
5. Enjoy.

POMEGRANATE
Pistachio
Couscous

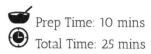

Prep Time: 10 mins
Total Time: 25 mins

Servings per Recipe: 6
Calories	276.3
Fat	11.6 g
Cholesterol	15.2 mg
Sodium	5.5 mg
Carbohydrates	38.0 g
Protein	6.3 g

Ingredients

1 C. couscous
2 C. fruit juice
2 tbsp. rose water
3 tbsp. melted sweet butter
1/4 C. finely ground blanched almond
1/4 C. finely ground pistachio nut
1/2 C. powdered sugar

1/2-1 tbsp. cinnamon
1 C. candy-covered almonds
1/2 C. pomegranate seeds

Directions

1. Place a large saucepan over medium heat. Combine in it the fruit juice with water.
2. Heat them until they start boiling. Stir in the couscous and put on the lid.
3. Turn off the heat and let them sit for 16 min. stir them with a fork. Stir in 3 tbsp. of butter.
4. Add the pistachios and almonds. Mix them well.
5. Spoon the mixture into serving plates. Garnish them with powdered sugar, cinnamon, candy almonds and pomegranate seeds.
6. Enjoy.

Roasted
COUSCOUS

🥣 Prep Time: 15 mins
🕐 Total Time: 50 mins

Servings per Recipe: 6
Calories	132.9
Fat	2.9 g
Cholesterol	8.8 mg
Sodium	223.4 mg
Carbohydrates	19.4 g
Protein	7.2 g

Ingredients

14 oz. reduced-sodium fat-free chicken broth
3/4 C. uncooked couscous
2 C. sliced yellow squash
1/2 C. sliced green onion
2 tbsp. chopped fresh basil
1 tbsp. chopped fresh oregano
1 garlic clove, minced

1/4 C. shredded Fontina cheese
1/4 C. grated parmesan cheese
1/4 C. egg substitute
1/4 tsp. salt
1/4 tsp. pepper

Directions

1. Before you do anything, preheat the oven to 400 F.
2. Place a pot over medium heat. Heat in it 1 C. of broth until it starts boiling.
3. Stir in the couscous and put on the lid. Turn off the heat and let it sit for 6 min.
4. Stir in it with a fork and place it aside.
5. Place a large pan over high heat. Coat it with a cooking spray.
6. Cook in it the squash, onions, basil, oregano, and garlic for 3 to 4 min while stirring.
7. Get a mixing bowl: Mix in it the fontina and parmesan cheese.
8. Get a large mixing bowl: Mix in it the cooked veggies with couscous and half the cheese mixture.
9. Add the rest of the broth, egg substitute, salt, and pepper. Combine them well.
10. Pour the mixture into a greased baking dish. Cook it in the oven for 26 to 36 min.
11. Allow your couscous casserole to cool down for a while then serve it warm.
12. Enjoy.

TURKISH
Inspired Couscous

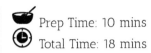

Prep Time: 10 mins
Total Time: 18 mins

Servings per Recipe: 3
Calories   419.4
Fat   14.1 g
Cholesterol   20.3 mg
Sodium   121.3 mg
Carbohydrates   64.2 g
Protein   10.9 g

Ingredients

1 C. couscous
2 C. fruit juice
2 tbsp. rose water
3 tbsp. melted sweet butter
1/4 C. finely ground blanched almond
1/4 C. finely ground pistachio nut
1/2 C. powdered sugar

1/2-1 tbsp. cinnamon
1 C. candy-covered almonds
1/2 C. pomegranate seeds

Directions

1. Get a large mixing bowl: Mix in it the couscous, stock powder, sugar and grated orange rind.
2. Stir in the boiling water and put on the lid. Let them sit for 5 to 6 min.
3. Place a small skillet over medium heat. Heat in it the butter until it melts.
4. Add the currants with nuts and cook them for 2 to 3 min. Stir in the apricots.
5. Add the mixture to the couscous and stir them well.
6. Garnish it with spring onions and coriander then serve it.
7. Enjoy.

Couscous
Masala

Prep Time: 10 mins
Total Time: 30 mins

Servings per Recipe: 4
Calories   274.4
Fat   10.4 g
Cholesterol   0.0 mg
Sodium   249.0 mg
Carbohydrates   37.1 g
Protein   7.9 g

Ingredients

2 tbsp. pine nuts
2 tbsp. olive oil
1 shallot, peeled and minced
1 carrot, peeled and coarsely shredded
2 tbsp. lemon juice
1 tbsp. garam masala, see appendix

1 1/4 C. chicken broth
1 C. Israeli couscous

Directions

1. Place a large pan over medium heat. Toast in it the pine nuts until they become golden brown.
2. Place them aside to cool down.
3. Place a pot over high heat. Heat in it the oil. Cook in it the shallot for 60 sec.
4. Add the lemon juice and garam masala. Cook them until they start boiling.
5. Add the couscous and low the heat. Put on the lid and let them cook for 9 min.
6. Once the time is up, turn off the heat and let them rest for 6 min.
7. Stir them with a fork. Transfer it to serving bowls.
8. Garnish them with toasted pine nuts and serve them.
9. Enjoy.

ISFAHAN
Bowls

🥣 Prep Time: 5 mins
🕐 Total Time: 35 mins

Servings per Recipe: 8
Calories   308.6
Fat   12.0 g
Cholesterol   6.0 mg
Sodium   125.7 mg
Carbohydrates   42.1 g
Protein   8.4 g

Ingredients

2 tbsp. sesame seeds
2 tbsp. pine nuts
1 tbsp. butter
1 small onion, finely diced
2 1/2 C. chicken stock
1 pinch saffron, crumbled
2 C. couscous
1/4 C. olive oil, extra virgin

1 lemon, juice of
1/2 tsp. red pepper flakes
1/4 C. sultana raisin
1 1/2 C. mixed herbs, finely chopped
kosher salt ground pepper
fresh ground pepper

Directions

1. Place a small pan over medium heat. Toast in it the pine nuts until they become golden brown.
2. Place them aside to cool down.
3. Place a small pan over high heat. Heat in it the butter until it melts.
4. Cook in it the onion for 7 to 8 min while stirring until it becomes golden.
5. Place a pot over medium-high heat. Stir in it the saffron with stock.
6. Heat them until they start boiling. Turn off the heat and stir in the couscous.
7. Put on the lid and let it sit for 16 min. stir it with a fork.
8. Add the oil, lemon juice, and red pepper flakes. Mix them well.
9. Stir in the sesame seeds, pine nuts, onions, raisins, herbs, a pinch of salt and pepper.
10. Serve your couscous warm or cold.
11. Enjoy.

Simple
Capsicum
Couscous

🥣 Prep Time: 10 mins
🕐 Total Time: 16 mins

Servings per Recipe: 4
Calories	204.6
Fat	3.7 g
Cholesterol	0.0 mg
Sodium	151.1 mg
Carbohydrates	36.1 g
Protein	5.8 g

Ingredients

1 tbsp. olive oil
1 small onion, finely chopped
1/2 red bell peppers, diced
1/4 tsp. dried thyme
1/4 tsp. salt
1/4 tsp. fresh black pepper

1 1/2 C. vegetable broth
1 C. couscous

Directions

1. Place a pot over medium heat. Heat in it the oil. Cook in it the onion, bell pepper, thyme, salt and pepper for 6 min.
2. Stir in the broth and cook them until they start boiling. Stir in the couscous and put on the lid.
3. Turn off the heat and let them sit for 6 min. Mix them with a fork.
4. Adjust the seasoning of your couscous then serve it cold or warm.
5. Enjoy.

COUSCOUS
Salad V (Honey Orange Glazed)

Prep Time: 10 mins
Total Time: 20 mins

Servings per Recipe: 6
Calories   221.2
Fat   3.3 g
Cholesterol   1.2 mg
Sodium   151.5 mg
Carbohydrates   41.7 g
Protein   6.5 g

Ingredients

1 C. chicken stock
1 C. couscous
1/2 tsp. curry powder
3/4 C. canned chick-peas, rinsed and drained
1/3 C. dried cranberries
1/4 C. green onion, chopped
1/4 C. red bell pepper, diced
1/4 C. fresh basil, chopped

Dressing
1 tbsp. olive oil
2 tbsp. thawed orange juice
2 tbsp. lemon juice
2 tsp. grated orange rind
3 tbsp. honey
1 tsp. minced garlic

Directions

1. Place a pot over medium heat. Heat in it the stock until it starts boiling.
2. Add the couscous with curry powder. Put on the lid and let them sit for 6 min.
3. Pour the mixture into a large mixing bowl.
4. Get a mixing bowl: Whisk in it the olive oil, orange juice, orange rind, honey, and garlic.
5. Add it to the couscous with chickpeas, cranberries, green onions, bell pepper, and basil.
6. Stir them well then serve them immediately.
7. Enjoy.

Dried
Apricot Couscous

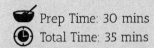 Prep Time: 30 mins

Total Time: 35 mins

Servings per Recipe: 4

Calories	402.7
Fat	12.9 g
Cholesterol	15.2 mg
Sodium	61.3 mg
Carbohydrates	63.0 g
Protein	9.5 g

Ingredients

9 oz. couscous
1 1/2 tbsp. olive oil
4 tsp. ras el hanout spice mix, see appendix
1 tsp. ground coriander, Cilantro
1 tsp. ground paprika
1 tsp. ground turmeric
1 tbsp. pine nuts, lightly toasted
6 - 8 soft dried apricots, chopped finely

2 tbsp. golden sultana raisins
1 tbsp. dried onion flakes
1 tbsp. garlic granules
1 C. hot vegetable stock
1-oz butter
2 tbsp. chopped fresh coriander, cilantro

Directions

1. Get a mixing bowl: Mix in in it the couscous with ras el hanout, coriander, paprika, turmeric, onion flakes, apricots, pine nuts, and sultana.
2. Mix into it the oil. Stir in the boiling stock and put on the lid.
3. Let them sit for 6 min. add the butter and mix them well.
4. Adjust the seasoning of your couscous then serve it warm.
5. Enjoy.

PRIYA'S
Couscous Madras

Prep Time: 10 mins
Total Time: 25 mins

Servings per Recipe: 4
Calories	479.8
Fat	25.8 g
Cholesterol	0.0 mg
Sodium	433.5 mg
Carbohydrates	53.5 g
Protein	11.0 g

Ingredients
1 1/2 C. chicken broth
1/2 C. golden raisin
1 tsp. curry powder
1/4 tsp. salt
1 C. uncooked couscous
1/3 C. oil
2 tbsp. lemon juice

1 tsp. sugar
1/2 C. slivered almonds, toasted
2 fresh green onions, sliced

Directions
1. Place a pot over medium heat. Stir in it the chicken broth, raisins, curry powder, and salt.
2. Heat them until they start boiling. Lower the heat and add the couscous.
3. Put on the lid and let them sit for 6 min. stir them with a fork.
4. Get a mixing bowl: Whisk in it the oil, lemon juice, sugar, and almonds.
5. Add it to the couscous and mix them well. Garnish it with some green onions then serve it.
6. Enjoy.

Couscous
Stew

Prep Time: 5 mins
Total Time: 35 mins

Servings per Recipe: 4
Calories	155.0
Fat	4.1 g
Cholesterol	0.0 mg
Sodium	443.1 mg
Carbohydrates	26.8 g
Protein	5.0 g

Ingredients

1 - 2 tbsp. olive oil
1 large onion, finely diced
1 tsp. cumin, ground
3 garlic cloves, crushed
30 oz. cans diced tomatoes
2.5 oz. tomato paste
4 C. vegetable stock

1/3 C. instant couscous
1/2 bunch fresh coriander, chopped
1/2 tsp. sea salt
1/2 tsp. fresh ground pepper

Directions

1. Place a pot over medium heat. Heat in it the oil.
2. Cook in it the onion for 8 min while stirring often.
3. Stir in the tomatoes, tomato paste, and stock. Cook them until they start boiling.
4. Lower the heat and let them cook for 16 min. Stir in the couscous and cook them for 8 min.
5. Adjust the seasoning of your couscous. Garnish it with coriander leaves then serve it warm.
6. Enjoy.

PENNSYLVANIA
Country Couscous

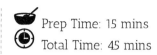

Prep Time: 15 mins
Total Time: 45 mins

Servings per Recipe: 5

Calories	512.2
Fat	8.1 g
Cholesterol	0.0 mg
Sodium	874.4 mg
Carbohydrates	99.1 g
Protein	15.4 g

Ingredients

1/4 C. sliced almonds, toasted
Squash
1 1/2 tbsp. olive oil
2 onions, chopped
2 garlic cloves, minced
1/4 tsp. cayenne pepper
1/8 tsp. grated nutmeg
1/8 tsp. cinnamon
1 C. canned diced tomatoes with juice
1 butternut squash, peeled, halved lengthwise, seeded, and cut into 3/4-inch dice

1/4 C. raisins
3 C. vegetable broth
1 tsp. salt
1 (14 1/2 oz) cans canned chick-peas, drained and rinsed
3/4 C. chopped fresh parsley, curly or flat leaf
Couscous
1 1/2-3 C. water
1 1/2 C. couscous
1/4 tsp. salt

Directions

1. To prepare the squash:
2. Place a large pot over low heat. Hat in it the oil.
3. Stir in the onion and cook it for 6 min while stirring often.
4. Add the tomatoes, squash, raisins, broth, and 1 tsp. of the salt.
5. Cook them until they start simmering. Add the chickpeas and put on the lid.
6. Cook them for 1 min. Remove the lid and let them cook for an extra 12 min.
7. Add the parsley and turn off the heat.
8. To prepare the couscous:
9. Place a large saucepan over medium heat.
10. Heat in it the water with 1/4 tsp. of salt. Heat them until they start boiling.
11. Add the couscous and put on the lid. Let it sit for 6 min.
12. Once the time is up, stir it with a fork then serve it with the squash stew Enjoy.

Tunisian
Couscous Hot Pot

🥣 Prep Time: 15 mins
🕐 Total Time: 29 mins

Servings per Recipe: 6
Calories   358.8
Fat   4.7 g
Cholesterol   0.0 mg
Sodium   781.0 mg
Carbohydrates   66.9 g
Protein   13.5 g

Ingredients
Stew
1 tbsp. olive oil
2 C. zucchini, cubed
1 C. onion, chopped
1/2 C. carrot, chopped
1 tbsp. garlic, minced
1 C. chicken broth
2 tbsp. raisins
1 1/4 tsp. ground ginger
1 1/4 tsp. ground cumin
3/4 tsp. ground coriander
1/2 tsp. salt

1/4 tsp. cinnamon
1/4 tsp. black pepper
2 (15 1/2 oz.) cans chickpeas, drained
1 (14 1/2 oz.) cans no-salt-added diced tomatoes, undrained
Couscous
1 1/2 C. water
1 C. uncooked couscous

Directions
1. To prepare the stew:
2. Place a large pan over high heat. Heat in it the oil.
3. Cook in it the zucchini, onion, carrot, and garlic for 6 min.
4. Add the broth with raisins, ginger, cumin, coriander, salt, cinnamon, chickpeas, and tomatoes.
5. Cook them until they start boiling. Put on the lid and lower the heat.
6. Cook them for 9 min while stirring often.
7. Pour the water into a saucepan and bring it to a boil.
8. Add the couscous and put on the lid. Turn off the heat and let it sit for 6 min.
9. Serve your couscous warm with the veggies stew then serve it hot.
10. Enjoy.

COUSCOUS
Kerala Style

Prep Time: 15 mins
Total Time: 30 mins

Servings per Recipe: 4
Calories	846.5
Fat	31.7 g
Cholesterol	78.3 mg
Sodium	177.9 mg
Carbohydrates	110.2 g
Protein	33.1 g

Ingredients

1 C. water
1 C. couscous
2 tbsp. olive oil
1 medium yellow onion, diced
3 garlic cloves, minced
2 large carrots, cut into matchsticks
1 C. golden raisin
1 tbsp. curry powder

2 lbs. rotisserie-cooked chicken, shredded
1 C. coconut milk
1 pinch salt, to taste
1 pinch pepper, to taste
3 scallions, thinly sliced

Directions

1. Place a medium saucepan over high heat. Heat in it the water until it starts boiling.
2. Stir in the couscous and put on the lid. Turn off the heat and put on the lid.
3. Let them sit for 5 to 6 min.
4. Place a large pan over medium heat. Heat in it the oil.
5. Cook in it the onion, garlic, carrots and raisins for 6 min.
6. Stir in the curry and cook them for 4 min while stirring.
7. Stir in the coconut milk with chicken. Cook them until they start simmering.
8. Stir in a pinch of salt and pepper. Serve your couscous warm with the chicken stew.
9. Enjoy.

Couscous
in February

Prep Time: 5 mins
Total Time: 19 mins

Servings per Recipe: 2
Calories	649.1
Fat	31.7 g
Cholesterol	85.1 mg
Sodium	613.5 mg
Carbohydrates	61.0 g
Protein	30.0 g

Ingredients

1/2 lb boneless chicken, cut into strips
1/8 tsp. salt
1/4 tsp. black pepper
2 tbsp. olive oil
2 tbsp. apricot preserves
1 tsp. balsamic vinegar
1 C. chicken broth

1/3 C. finely chopped dried apricot
1/2 C. uncooked couscous

Directions

1. To prepare the stew:
2. Place a large pan over high heat. Heat in it the oil.
3. Cook in it the zucchini, onion, carrot, and garlic for 6 min.
4. Add the broth with raisins, ginger, cumin, coriander, salt, cinnamon, chickpeas, and tomatoes.
5. Cook them until they start boiling. Put on the lid and lower the heat.
6. Cook them for 9 min while stirring often.
7. Pour the water into a saucepan and bring it to a boil.
8. Add the couscous and put on the lid. Turn off the heat and let it sit for 6 min.
9. Serve your couscous warm with the veggies stew then serve it hot.
10. Enjoy.

HOW TO MAKE
Couscous

Prep Time: 5 mins
Total Time: 17 mins

Servings per Recipe: 4
Calories	298.9
Fat	5.4 g
Cholesterol	11.4 mg
Sodium	90.1 mg
Carbohydrates	51.7 g
Protein	11.0 g

Ingredients

1 1/2 C. low sodium chicken broth
1/4 C. water
2 carrots, minced
1 C. shelled fresh peas
1 1/4 C. couscous
3 tbsp. fresh lemon juice

1 1/2 tbsp. grated lemon peel
1 1/2 tbsp. butter
salt and pepper, to taste

Directions

1. Place a small pot over high heat. Heat in it the broth with water until they start boiling.
2. Stir in the carrots and cook them for 3 min. Stir in the peas and cook them for 5 min.
3. Stir in the couscous and cook them for half a minute.
4. Stir in the lemon juice, lemon peel, and butter. Mix them until the butter melts.
5. Turn off the heat and put on the lid. Let them sit for 6 min.
6. Adjust the seasoning of your couscous then serve it warm.
7. Enjoy.

Fragrant
Couscous

Prep Time: 10 mins
Total Time: 20 mins

Servings per Recipe: 4
Calories   358.2
Fat   12.4 g
Cholesterol   0.0 mg
Sodium   285.8 mg
Carbohydrates   52.2 g
Protein   8.7 g

Ingredients

1 1/2 tsp. garlic, minced
3 tbsp. olive oil
1 3/4 C. vegetable broth
1/4 tsp. salt
1 1/2 C. couscous
16 black olives, pitted and coarsely chopped

1/2 C. flat leaf parsley, chopped
1 1/2 tsp. lemon zest, finely grated

Directions

1. Place a large pot over high heat. Heat in it the oil.
2. Cook in it the garlic for 1 min. Stir in the water with salt.
3. Heat them until they start boiling. Add the rest of the ingredients.
4. Put on the lid and turn off the heat. Let them sit for 6 min.
5. Adjust the seasoning of your couscous then serve it.
6. Enjoy.

COUSCOUS
Salad 101

🍲 Prep Time: 20 mins
🕐 Total Time: 1 hr 20 mins

Servings per Recipe: 7
Calories	221.1
Fat	8.0 g
Cholesterol	0.0 mg
Sodium	113.6 mg
Carbohydrates	31.9 g
Protein	6.2 g

Ingredients
1 1/3 C. water
1 C. couscous, uncooked
1 (11 oz.) cans mandarin oranges, drained
1 C. frozen peas, thawed
1/2 C. slivered almonds, toasted
1/3 C. red onion, chopped

3 tbsp. cider vinegar
2 tbsp. olive oil
1 tbsp. sugar
1/4 tsp. salt
1/4 tsp. hot pepper sauce

Directions
1. Place a large saucepan over high heat. Heat in it the water until it starts boiling.
2. Add the couscous and put on the lid. Turn off the heat and let them sit for 6 min.
3. Stir it with a fork and let it cool down for 60 min in the fridge.
4. Get a mixing bowl: Place in it the oranges, peas, almonds, onion, and couscous.
5. Get a mixing bowl: Whisk in it the vinegar, oil, sugar, salt and hot pepper sauce.
6. Add it to the couscous mixture and mix them well. Serve it immediately.
7. Enjoy.

Oriental
House Fried Couscous

🍲 Prep Time: 10 mins
🕐 Total Time: 30 mins

Servings per Recipe: 6
Calories	114.5
Fat	0.2 g
Cholesterol	0.0 mg
Sodium	340.1 mg
Carbohydrates	23.2 g
Protein	4.3 g

Ingredients

vegetable oil
1/2 scallion, sliced
1 1/2 C. water
2 tbsp. soy sauce
1/2 tsp. sugar
1/4 tsp. ground ginger
1/4 tsp. garlic powder

1/8-1/4 tsp. cayenne pepper
1 C. couscous, uncooked

Directions

1. Place a large saucepan over high heat. Grease it with some oil.
2. Cook in it the scallions for 2 min. Stir in the water with soy sauce sugar, ginger, garlic and cayenne pepper.
3. Cook them until they start boiling. Turn off the heat and stir in the couscous.
4. Put on the lid and let them sit for 6 min. stir it with a fork then serve it.
5. Enjoy.

HOT CAPRESE
Style Couscous

Prep Time: 30 mins
Total Time: 1 hr 30 mins

Servings per Recipe: 8
Calories	166.0
Fat	7.0 g
Cholesterol	0.0 mg
Sodium	7.2 mg
Carbohydrates	22.2 g
Protein	3.8 g

Ingredients

7 oz. couscous
1 red chili pepper, seeded and finely chopped
8 oz. cherry tomatoes, quartered
1 bunch green onion, sliced
4 tbsp. extra virgin olive oil
2 tbsp. lemon juice
4 tbsp. cilantro, freshly chopped

salt, to taste
fresh ground pepper, to taste

Directions

1. Get a mixing bowl: Place in it the couscous. Cover it with 1 C. of boiling water.
2. Put on the lid and let it sit for 35 min.
3. Get a mixing bowl: Whisk in it the olive oil with cilantro and lemon juice.
4. Pour the mixture over the couscous followed by the chili pepper, tomatoes, onion, a pinch of salt and pepper.
5. Place the couscous pot in the fridge and let it sit for 60 min then serve it.
6. Enjoy.

Couscous Mendoza

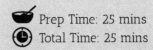
Prep Time: 25 mins
Total Time: 25 mins

Servings per Recipe: 8
Calories	457.0
Fat	14.5 g
Cholesterol	11.4 mg
Sodium	102.8 mg
Carbohydrates	69.2 g
Protein	14.5 g

Ingredients

3 tbsp. butter
3 tbsp. olive oil
3 medium onions, finely chopped
1 tsp. brown sugar
1 tbsp. fresh minced garlic
1 pinch cayenne pepper
3 tsp. turmeric
2 tsp. cumin

1 - 2 tsp. fresh ground black pepper
3 C. couscous
6 C. hot low sodium chicken broth
3/4 C. currants
1/2 C. slivered almonds
seasoning salt

Directions

1. Place a large saucepan over high heat. Heat in it the broth until it starts boiling.
2. Place a large pan over high heat. Heat in it the oil with butter until it melts.
3. Stir in the onion with 1 tsp. of sugar. Cook them for 14 min while stirring them often.
4. Stir in the garlic, cayenne, turmeric, cumin and ground black pepper. Cook them for 2 to 3 min.
5. Stir in the couscous with caramelized onion. Add the boiling broth with currants.
6. Put on the lid and turn off the heat. Let them sit for 14 min.
7. Stir your couscous with a fork. Adjust its seasoning then garnish it with some almonds.
8. Enjoy.

ENGLISH
Cucumber
Couscous

Prep Time: 10 mins
Total Time: 10 mins

Servings per Recipe: 8
Calories   202.3
Fat   5.2 g
Cholesterol   13.4 mg
Sodium   467.5 mg
Carbohydrates   31.4 g
Protein   7.3 g

Ingredients

2 C. water
1 tbsp. olive oil
1 tsp. salt
1 garlic clove, minced
1 (10 oz.) boxes couscous
1-pint grape tomatoes or 1-pint cherry tomatoes halved
1 1/2 C. diced English cucumbers
1/3 C. chopped green onion

1/3 C. fresh lemon juice
2 tbsp. chopped of fresh mint
1 tbsp. chopped fresh dill
4 oz. feta cheese, crumbled

Directions

1. Place a large saucepan over high heat. Combine in it the water with oil, salt, and garlic.
2. Heat them until they start boiling. Add the couscous and turn off the heat.
3. Put on the lid and let them sit for 6 min. Stir them with a fork and let them cool down.
4. Transfer the couscous mixture to a mixing bowl. Add to it the remaining ingredients.
5. Mix them well then top it with cheese and serve it.
6. Enjoy.

Sousous's
COUSCOUS

Prep Time: 10 mins
Total Time: 35 mins

Servings per Recipe: 8
Calories	214.5
Fat	10.9 g
Cholesterol	0.0 mg
Sodium	10.9 mg
Carbohydrates	23.9 g
Protein	5.3 g

Ingredients

1/2 C. red onion, chopped finely
1/4 C. lemon juice
2 tbsp. apple cider vinegar
1 C. lentils
5 C. water
1/3 C. extra virgin olive oil, plus
1 tbsp. extra virgin olive oil
1 C. couscous

4 tbsp. fresh parsley, chopped
4 tbsp. of fresh mint, chopped
3 scallions, white and light green part only, sliced thin
salt and pepper

Directions

1. Get a mixing bowl: Mix in it the red onion, lemon juice and vinegar with a pinch of salt.
2. Place a large pot over high heat. Combine in it 4 C. of with lentils.
3. Cook them until they start boiling. Lower the heat and cook it for 22 min.
4. Once the time is up, turn off the heat and let it cool down for 6 min.
5. Strain the lentils and transfer them to a mixing bowl.
6. Add to them 1/3 C. of olive oil with lemon mix and stir them well.
7. Place a large saucepan over high heat. Heat in it 1 C. of water until it starts boiling.
8. Stir in the couscous and put on the lid. Turn off the heat and let it sit for 6 min.
9. Stir it with a fork. Add 1 tbsp. of olive oil and mix them well.
10. Transfer it to a serving plate. Top it with the lentils, parsley, mint, and scallions.
11. Serve it immediately.
12. Enjoy.

THURSDAY
Night Couscous

Prep Time: 10 mins
Total Time: 20 mins

Servings per Recipe: 4
Calories   308.9
Fat   7.2 g
Cholesterol   0.0 mg
Sodium   301.1 mg
Carbohydrates   51.5 g
Protein   8.4 g

Ingredients

2 tbsp. olive oil
2 garlic cloves, minced
1/2 tsp. turmeric
1 2/3 C. water
1 tsp. lemon zest, finely grated
1/2 tsp. coarse salt

1 1/2 C. couscous
1/4 C. fresh cilantro, chopped
2 tbsp. fresh lemon juice
salt and pepper, to taste

Directions

1. Place a pot over high heat. Heat in it the oil.
2. Cook in it the garlic with turmeric for 1 to 2 min.
3. Stir in the water, lemon zest, and coarse salt. Heat them until they start boiling.
4. Turn off the heat and add the couscous. Put on the lid and let it sit for 6 min.
5. Mix them with a fork. Add the cilantro with lemon juice, a pinch of salt and pepper.
6. Mix them well then serve it immediately.
7. Enjoy.

5-Ingredient
Tampa Style Couscous

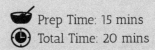 Prep Time: 15 mins
Total Time: 20 mins

Servings per Recipe: 4
Calories   305.2
Fat   3.8 g
Cholesterol   0.0 mg
Sodium   10.9 mg
Carbohydrates   56.9 g
Protein   9.1 g

Ingredients

2 C. water
5 -6 tbsp. orange juice
1 tbsp. olive oil
1 tsp. orange zest, grated

1 (10 oz.) boxes couscous

Directions

1. Place a pot over medium heat. Stir in it the water with 2 tbsp. of orange juice olive oil and orange zest.
2. Heat them until they start boiling. Add the couscous and put on the lid.
3. Turn off the heat and let them sit for 14 min. Stir them with a fork then add the orange juice.
4. Serve it warm or cold.
5. Enjoy.

A LIGHT
Couscous Bronzer

🥣 Prep Time: 20 mins
🕐 Total Time: 31 mins

Servings per Recipe: 4
Calories   348.8
Fat   1.6 g
Cholesterol   0.0 mg
Sodium   328.2 mg
Carbohydrates   73.5 g
Protein   11.5 g

Ingredients
2 C. water
1 1/2 tsp. lemon zest, grated
2 tbsp. of lemon juice
2 tbsp. garlic oil
1/2 tsp. ground cinnamon
1 C. couscous

1 (15 oz.) cans garbanzo beans, rinsed and drained
1/2 C. golden raisin
salt and pepper

Directions
1. Place a medium saucepan over high heat.
2. Combine in it 2 C. of water with lemon juice, garlic oil, and ground cinnamon.
3. Heat them until they start boiling. Lower the heat and cook them for 2 min.
4. Turn off the heat and add the couscous. Put on the lid and let it sit for 6 min.
5. Add the garbanzo beans, golden raisins, and reserved lemon peel. Mix them well.
6. Put on the lid and let them sit for an extra 6 min.
7. Once the time is up, adjust the seasoning of your couscous then serve it.
8. Enjoy.

Peter's
COUSCOUS

🥄 Prep Time: 10 mins
🕐 Total Time: 25 mins

Servings per Recipe: 16
Calories   112.6
Fat   6.9 g
Cholesterol   0.0 mg
Sodium   367.2 mg
Carbohydrates   12.3 g
Protein   2.1 g

Ingredients
4 1/2 C. water
1/4 C. extra-virgin olive oil
3 cinnamon sticks, halved
1 1/2 tsp. ground cumin
2 1/2 tsp. coarse salt
1 C. chopped dried apricot
Two 10-oz boxes couscous (about 3 1/4 C.)

3/4 C. dried currant
1 C. shelled natural pistachios, toasted lightly, cooled, and chopped coarse
3 tbsp. chopped fresh mint leaves

Directions
1. Place a large pot over high heat. Stir in it the water, oil, cinnamon, cumin, salt, and apricots.
2. Cook them until they start boiling. Stir in the couscous and put on the lid.
3. Let them sit for 6 min. stir them with a fork then transfer the mixture to a large pan.
4. Allow it to cool down completely. Garnish it with some pistachios, currants and mint leaves.
5. Enjoy.

COUSCOUS
Ballads

Prep Time: 5 mins
Total Time: 10 mins

Servings per Recipe: 4
Calories	191.8
Fat	6.2 g
Cholesterol	7.6 mg
Sodium	433.6 mg
Carbohydrates	26.9 g
Protein	6.6 g

Ingredients

3/4 C. couscous
1 C. chicken broth
1 tbsp. butter
1/4 C. sliced almonds, toasted
2 tbsp. cilantro, chopped

1 tbsp. orange zest, chopped
1/2 tsp. kosher salt

Directions

1. Place a large saucepan over high heat. Heat in it the broth until it starts boiling.
2. Add the butter and couscous. Put on the lid and turn off the heat.
3. Let it sit for 6 min. Stir it with a fork then add the almonds, cilantro, orange zest, and salt.
4. Adjust the seasoning of your couscous then serve it warm or cold.
5. Enjoy.

Indian
Meets Mediterranean Couscous

Prep Time: 20 mins
Total Time: 27 mins

Servings per Recipe: 6
Calories	705.4
Fat	39.6 g
Cholesterol	33.3 mg
Sodium	1149.3 mg
Carbohydrates	68.7 g
Protein	23.1 g

Ingredients
1 -2 tbsp. curry powder
2 1/4 C. water
1 tsp. salt
7 C. broccoli, small florets
1 large carrot, sliced paper thin
1 (10 oz.) boxes couscous
1 (15 oz.) cans chickpeas, well drained and rinsed
1/2 C. olive oil
1/4 C. white vinegar
1 tbsp. minced fresh ginger
1 1/2 C. feta cheese, crumbled
4 -5 green onions, chopped
1 C. sliced almonds, toasted
salt and pepper

Directions
1. Place a pot over high heat. Toast in it the curry powder for 60 sec.
2. Stir in 2-1/4 C. water with 1 tsp. salt with the broccoli and carrots.
3. Cook them until they start boiling. Put on the lid and cook them for an extra minute.
4. Turn off the heat and add the couscous. Put on the lid and let it sit for 6 min.
5. Transfer the mixture to a large mixing bowl. Add the garbanzo beans, oil, vinegar, minced fresh ginger.
6. Mix them well. Stir in the feta cheese with almonds, green onions, a pinch of salt and pepper.
7. Serve your couscous warm or cold.
8. Enjoy.

RED CHILI
and Coriander
Couscous

Prep Time: 10 mins
Total Time: 15 mins

Servings per Recipe: 1	
Calories	1633.3
Fat	69.2 g
Cholesterol	10.6 mg
Sodium	560.1 mg
Carbohydrates	211.1 g
Protein	48.5 g

Ingredients
2 tbsp. olive oil
1 garlic clove, finely chopped
1 tbsp. ground cumin
1 tsp. ground coriander
1 tsp. paprika
1 1/4 C. chicken stock
good pinch saffron strand

6 spring onions, trimmed and thinly sliced
8 oz. couscous
1 lemon, juice and zest of
2 red chili, seeded and finely chopped
1.5 oz. pine nuts, toasted

Directions
1. Place a large saucepan over high heat. Heat in it 1 tbsp. of oil.
2. Stir in it the cumin, garlic, coriander, and paprika. Cook them for 60 sec while stirring.
3. Stir in the saffron and stock. Heat them until they start boiling.
4. Stir in the spring onion with couscous. Put on the lid and turn off the heat.
5. Let them sit for 6 min. Add the remaining oil and mix them well with a fork.
6. Serve your couscous warm or cold.
7. Enjoy.

Persian
Palace Couscous

Prep Time: 20 mins
Total Time: 1 hr 20 mins

Servings per Recipe: 6
Calories	182.2
Fat	0.8 g
Cholesterol	0.0 mg
Sodium	152.0 mg
Carbohydrates	37.2 g
Protein	5.7 g

Ingredients
1 1/2 C. water
3/8 tsp. saffron thread
3/4 tsp. extra virgin olive oil
3/8 tsp. salt
1 1/2 C. couscous

1/4 C. raisins
2 1/4 tbsp. chopped of fresh mint

Directions
1. Place a large saucepan over high heat. Heat in it the water until it starts boiling.
2. Stir in the saffron. Put on the lid and turn off the heat.
3. Let it sit for 35 min. bring it to a boil once again.
4. Stir in the olive oil, salt, couscous, and raisins. Turn off the heat and put on the lid.
5. Let them sit for 35 min. Stir the couscous with a fork.
6. Adjust the seasoning of your couscous then garnish it with mint.
7. Enjoy.

MS. FATHIA'S
Pudding

Prep Time: 10 mins
Total Time: 20 mins

Servings per Recipe: 4
Calories	517.0
Fat	20.4 g
Cholesterol	0.0 mg
Sodium	65.6 mg
Carbohydrates	79.0 g
Protein	7.5 g

Ingredients

3/4 C. couscous
3/4 C. coconut
1 tbsp. corn flour
3/4 C. soymilk
3/4 C. coconut milk, lite
1/4 C. golden syrup

1/2 tsp. mixed spice
yogurt, to serve

Directions

1. Get a large bowl: Combine in it the coconut with couscous.
2. Stir in 1 1/2 C. of boiling water. Put on the lid and let them sit for 6 min.
3. Place a large saucepan over high heat. Combine in it the corn flour, spices, milk, and syrup.
4. Mix them well while cooking until the mixture becomes thick.
5. Stir it into the couscous and let it chill for 35 min. Garnish it with some nuts and serve it with some yogurt.
6. Enjoy.

Autumn Root Vegetable Couscous

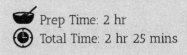

Prep Time: 2 hr
Total Time: 2 hr 25 mins

Servings per Recipe: 8
Calories   710.5
Fat   31.0 g
Cholesterol   74.4 mg
Sodium   213.1 mg
Carbohydrates   78.5 g
Protein   28.2 g

Ingredients
8 lamb chops
1 large onion, chopped
3 garlic cloves, minced
2 medium carrots, diced
2 medium courgettes (zucchini)
2 large potatoes, diced
1/4 swede (rutabaga)
1 parsnip
2 - 3 stalks celery, chopped
1 C. chickpeas, drained
2 tsp. ras el hanout spice mix, see appendix
salt & pepper

1 pinch dried mint
1/2 tbsp. sunflower oil
1 C. of tinned plum tomato, liquidized
6 C. water
1 large green chili pepper
17.5 oz. medium couscous
1 tbsp. ghee (clarified butter)
1 1/2 tbsp. margarine
1 glass water
olive oil

Directions
1. Place a large skillet over medium heat. Heat in it a splash of olive oil.
2. Stir in the onion with garlic, ras el hanout and chicken. Cook them for 4 min while stirring.
3. Stir in the carrots with courgette, parsnips, and celery. Cover them with 4 C. of water.
4. Stir in a pinch of salt and pepper then bring them to a boil. Lower the heat and let them cook for 45 min with the lid on.
5. Stir in the tomatoes, chickpeas and dried mint and 2 C. of water.
6. Cook them for an extra 35 min with the lid on.
7. Prepare the couscous by following the instructions on the package.
8. Serve your couscous hot with your meat stew.
9. Enjoy.

HABIBA'S
Favorite

Prep Time: 1 hr
Total Time: 1 hr 5 mins

Servings per Recipe: 4
Calories	513.8
Fat	28.5 g
Cholesterol	173.7 mg
Sodium	1019.9 mg
Carbohydrates	39.9 g
Protein	26.4 g

Ingredients

1 lb. large shrimp, peeled and deveined
1 tbsp. olive oil
4 garlic cloves, minced
1 tsp. dried tarragon, crushed
1/2 tsp. dried thyme, crushed
1/4 tsp. Old Bay Seasoning
1/2 C. pine nuts, toasted
1 (5 5/8 oz.) packages couscous

1 1/4 C. chicken broth
2/3 C. sliced green onion
1/3 C. lemon juice
1/4 C. melted butter
1 (6 oz.) packages Baby Spinach
shredded parmesan cheese

Directions

1. Get a ziplock bag: Place in it the shrimp with oil, garlic, tarragon, thyme and Old Bay seasoning.
2. Seal the bag and shake it to coat. Let it sit for 60 min in the fridge.
3. Cook the couscous by following the instructions on the package.
4. Add to it the onions with pine nuts. Mix them well.
5. Get a mixing bowl: Mix in it the butter with lemon juice.
6. Place a large pan over medium heat. Pour in it the shrimp with its marinade.
7. Cook it for 4 to 6 min while stirring. Stir in half of the lemon butter mix and cook them for an extra minute.
8. Arrange the spinach leaves in serving bowls. Pour over them the couscous followed by shrimp.
9. Garnish it with the rest of the lemon butter then serve it.
10. Enjoy.

West Indian
House Couscous

Prep Time: 15 mins
Total Time: 25 mins

Servings per Recipe: 8
Calories   371.0
Fat   11.4 g
Cholesterol   110.4 mg
Sodium   334.8 mg
Carbohydrates   51.5 g
Protein   17.6 g

Ingredients

1 lb. cleaned and peeled grilled shrimp
1 tsp. olive oil
1 tsp. soy sauce
1 tbsp. marmalade
2 tbsp. olive oil
1/4 C. sweet onion
1 clove garlic, minced
1/4 inch fresh ginger, minced
2 tbsp. Worcestershire sauce
1 C. chicken broth
1 C. passion fruit or pineapple

2/3 C. citrus marmalade
1/2 lb. couscous
1 dash cayenne pepper
1 tsp. freshly grated orange zest
1/2 C. dry roasted macadamias, coarsely crushed
1/4 C. dried cranberries
3 tbsp. finely chopped fresh parsley
salt and pepper

Directions

1. Get a large mixing bowl: Combine in it the shrimp with olive oil, soy sauce, and marmalade.
2. Put on the lid and let it sit for 20 min.
3. Before you do anything, preheat the grill and grease it.
4. Grill the shrimp for 3 to 4 min on each side. Place them aside to cool down.
5. Place a pot over high heat. Heat in it the oil. Cook in it the onion, ginger, and garlic for 4 min.
6. Add the Worcestershire sauce, stock, juice marmalade and cayenne pepper.
7. Cook them until they start boiling. Add the couscous with orange zest.
8. Put on the lid and turn off the heat. Let it sit for 12 min.
9. Once the time is up, stir in the nuts, dried cranberries, herbs, and shrimp.
10. Chill your couscous in the fridge for at least 10 min then serve it.
11. Enjoy.

West Indian House Couscous   53

FLORIDA
Sunshine
Couscous

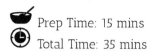

Prep Time: 15 mins
Total Time: 35 mins

Servings per Recipe: 6
Calories	441.7
Fat	14.8 g
Cholesterol	0.0 mg
Sodium	184.5 mg
Carbohydrates	65.8 g
Protein	13.4 g

Ingredients

1 tbsp. oil
1 C. almonds, coarsely chopped
1 onion, chopped
1/2 green pepper, chopped
2 C. orange juice
2 cinnamon sticks
5 cloves, whole
1/4 tsp. turmeric

1/4 tsp. ground red pepper
1/4 tsp. salt
1/4 tsp. pepper
2 C. couscous
1/4 C. raisins
1/2 C. green onion, chopped

Directions

1. Place a large pan over high heat. Heat in it the oil. Toast in it the almonds until they become golden.
2. Place them aside. Stir the green pepper with onion into the same pan. Cook them for 3 min.
3. Stir in the orange juice, cinnamon sticks, cloves, and spices. Cook them until they start boiling.
4. Add the raisins with couscous. Put on the lid and turn off the heat.
5. Let it sit for 6 min. Stir it with a fork then serve it.
6. Enjoy.

My First
COUSCOUS

🥣 Prep Time: 15 mins
🕐 Total Time: 45 mins

Servings per Recipe: 4
Calories	690.7
Fat	21.5 g
Cholesterol	118.2 mg
Sodium	2322.2 mg
Carbohydrates	80.3 g
Protein	42.5 g

Ingredients
2 tbsp. olive oil
8 chicken drumsticks
3 tsp. salt
1/4 tsp. fresh ground black pepper
1 onion, thin slices
1 turnip, peeled and 1/2 inch cubes
2 tbsp. tomato paste
1 tsp. paprika
1 1/2 tsp. ground cumin

1/8 tsp. cayenne
6 C. water
3 carrots, 1/4 inch slices
1 (15 oz.) cans chickpeas (1 2/3 C.)
1/2 C. flat leaf parsley, chopped and packed in
1 1/3 C. couscous

Directions
1. Place a large skillet over high heat. Heat in it the oil.
2. Season the chicken drumsticks with some salt and pepper. Brown them in the hot oil for 9 min while flipping them.
3. Drain them and place them aside. Keep only 1 tbsp. of fat in the pan and lower the heat.
4. Stir in the turnip with onion for cook them for 3 to 4 min.
5. Add the tomato paste, paprika, cumin, cayenne, and 2 1/4 tsp. of the salt. Cook them for 2 min.
6. Add the carrots with 4 C. of water. Stir in the chicken drumsticks and cook them until they start simmering.
7. Put on the lid and let them cook for 22 min. Add the parsley with chickpeas.
8. Cook them for an extra 6 min.
9. Place a large saucepan over high heat. Heat in it 2 C. of water until they start boiling.
10. Stir in the couscous with 1/4 tsp. of salt. Put on the lid and turn off the heat.
11. Let them sit for 6 min. Stir them with a fork.
12. Serve your couscous warm with the chicken stew then serve it hot.
13. Enjoy.

MOROCCAN
Drumsticks with Couscous

Prep Time: 5 mins
Total Time: 30 mins

Servings per Recipe: 4
Calories	639.8
Fat	24.7 g
Cholesterol	138.6 mg
Sodium	175.2 mg
Carbohydrates	65.7 g
Protein	39.2 g

Ingredients
4 whole chicken legs, cut into leg and thigh pieces
2 tsp. ground cinnamon, divided
1 tsp. ground ginger, divided
1 tbsp. olive oil
1 C. chopped onion
3/4 C. mixed chopped dried fruit (such as currants, apricots, and prunes)

1 (14 oz) cans low sodium chicken broth
1 C. couscous
2 tsp. finely chopped of fresh mint, divided

Directions
1. Before you do anything, preheat the oven to 375 F.
2. Season the chicken legs with 1 tsp. of cinnamon, 1/2 tsp. of ginger, salt, and pepper.
3. Place a large ovenproof pan over high heat. Heat in it the oil.
4. Brown in it the chicken legs for 9 min. Drain them and place them aside.
5. Transfer the pan to the oven and let them cook for 16 min.
6. Drain them and transfer them to a plate. Cover them with a piece of foil and place them aside.
7. Place the pan back over medium heat. Cook in it the onion for 6 min.
8. Stir in the dry fruit with 1 tsp. of cinnamon and 1/2 tsp. of ginger.
9. Stir in the broth and heat them until they start boiling.
10. Turn off the heat and add the couscous with 1 tsp. of mint. Put on the lid and let sit for 1 tsp. of mint.
11. Adjust the seasoning of your couscous then transfer it to a plate.
12. Top it with the roasted chicken then serve it warm.
13. Enjoy.

Braised
COUSCOUS

Prep Time: 10 mins
Total Time: 20 mins

Servings per Recipe: 3
Calories   320.0
Fat   8.9 g
Cholesterol   10.1 mg
Sodium   43.4 mg
Carbohydrates   50.7 g
Protein   8.9 g

Ingredients

1 C. couscous
1 1/2 C. vegetable broth
1 tbsp. olive oil
1 tbsp. butter
1 medium onion, diced
2 garlic cloves, pressed
1/2 red bell pepper, diced

1 - 2 C. sliced mushrooms
1 tbsp. pine nuts
2 tbsp. chives, finely chopped
salt
pepper

Directions

1. Place a large saucepan over high heat. Heat in it 1 1/2 C. of broth until it starts boiling.
2. Stir in the couscous and bring them to a boil. Put on the lid and turn off the heat.
3. Let it sit for 6 min.
4. Place a large skillet over high heat. Heat in it the olive oil.
5. Cook in it the mushroom with onion, a pinch of salt and pepper for 3 min.
6. Stir in the bell peppers with garlic. Cook them for 6 min.
7. Add the couscous and mix them with a fork. Transfer it to a plate and garnish it with pine nuts and chives.
8. Enjoy.

GLAZED COUSCOUS
with Maple Dressing

Prep Time: 20 mins
Total Time: 40 mins

Servings per Recipe: 4
Calories   687.6
Fat   29.1 g
Cholesterol   0.0 mg
Sodium   304.4 mg
Carbohydrates   89.5 g
Protein   19.1 g

Ingredients

2 tbsp. olive oil
2 C. Israeli couscous
4 C. low sodium chicken broth
1/4 C. fresh flat-leaf parsley, chopped
1 1/2 tbsp. fresh rosemary leaves, chopped
1 tsp. fresh thyme leave, chopped
1 medium green apple, diced
1 C. dried cranberries

1/2 C. slivered almonds, toasted
Dressing
1/4 C. apple cider vinegar
2 - 3 tbsp. maple syrup
1/2-1 tsp. kosher salt
1/2 tsp. fresh ground black pepper
1/4 C. olive oil

Directions

1. Place a large saucepan over high heat. Heat in it the olive oil.

2. Stir in the couscous and cook it for 4 min while stirring. Stir in the broth and cook them until they start boiling.

3. Lower the heat and let it cook for 10 to 1 min. Pour the mixture into a large bowl and let it cool down.

4. Stir in the parsley, rosemary, thyme, apple, dried cranberries, and almonds.

5. Get a mixing bowl: Whisk in it the vinegar, maple syrup, salt, and pepper.

6. Add the olive oil and mix them well. Drizzle it over the couscous and toss them to coat.

7. Adjust the seasoning of your couscous then serve it.

8. Enjoy.

Mexicana Couscous

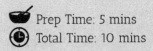
Prep Time: 5 mins
Total Time: 10 mins

Servings per Recipe: 2
Calories   318.6
Fat   4.2 g
Cholesterol   7.5 mg
Sodium   555.3 mg
Carbohydrates   57.4 g
Protein   11.8 g

Ingredients

1 1/2 tsp. butter
1 shallot, minced
1 C. chicken broth
3/4 C. couscous
1/3 C. fresh corn
1/4 tsp. pepper
1 pinch cayenne
1/8 tsp. salt

Directions

1. Place a large saucepan over high heat. Heat in it the butter until it melts.
2. Cook in it the shallot for 2 min while stirring. Stir in the broth and heat them until they start boiling.
3. Stir in the couscous, corn, pepper, cayenne, and salt.
4. Put on the lid and let it sits for 6 min. stir it with a fork then serve it.
5. Enjoy.

CAPRESE
COUSCOUS

🍲 Prep Time: 10 mins
🕐 Total Time: 10 mins

Servings per Recipe: 4
Calories   533.1
Fat   20.2 g
Cholesterol   15.9 mg
Sodium   321.3 mg
Carbohydrates   70.5 g
Protein   16.0 g

Ingredients

2 C. cooked couscous
1/2 C. crushed tomatoes
1 clove garlic, minced
1/4 salt
3 oz. gorgonzola
1 tsp. Dijon mustard
1/4 C. virgin olive oil
1/8 C. white balsamic vinegar

pepper
1 tbsp. fresh basil, chopped
fresh herbs, mixed with
fresh greens
1 small red onion, sliced very thinly

Directions

1. Get a blender: Combine in it the garlic, salt, gorgonzola cheese, mustard.
2. Blend them smooth. Add the oil and balsamic vinegar gradually in a steady stream. Blend them smooth.
3. Get a large mixing bowl: Place in it the couscous with tomatoes and the vinegar dressing.
4. Sprinkle the basil with pepper on top and mix them well.
5. Garnish your couscous with some greens then serve it.
6. Enjoy.

Lemon Raisin Couscous

🥣 Prep Time: 10 mins
🕐 Total Time: 20 mins

Servings per Recipe: 4
Calories   386.6
Fat   13.5 g
Cholesterol   1.8 mg
Sodium   158.7 mg
Carbohydrates   57.1 g
Protein   11.9 g

Ingredients

1 C. couscous
1 tbsp. olive oil
1 C. boiling chicken stock
1 tbsp. preserved lemon, finely chopped
1/2 C. parsley, finely chopped
1/2 C. mint, finely chopped
1/2 C. sultana (raisins)

1/2 C. almonds, roughly chopped, toasted
salt and pepper

Directions

1. Get a mixing bowl: Mix in the couscous with olive oil. Add the boiling stock and put on the lid.
2. Let it sit for 6 min then mix it with a fork.
3. Add the preserved lemon, mint, parsley, sultanas, almonds, a pinch of salt and pepper.
4. Mix them well then serve it.
5. Enjoy.

HOT AFRICAN
COUSCOUS

Prep Time: 5 mins
Total Time: 20 mins

Servings per Recipe: 2

Calories	336.1
Fat	2.9 g
Cholesterol	97.5 mg
Sodium	588.2 mg
Carbohydrates	55.4 g
Protein	21.6 g

Ingredients

100 g couscous
olive oil, for frying
200 ml chicken stock, fresh
1 small onion, sliced
2 garlic cloves, crushed
1 tsp. ground cumin

400 g chopped tomatoes
1 - 2 tsp. harissa, see appendix
150 g raw peeled prawns
1 small bunch coriander leaves

Directions

1. Mix the couscous with 1 tsp. of olive oil in a mixing bowl.
2. Add to it the boiling stock and put on the lid. Let it sit for 6 min.
3. Place a large skillet over high heat. Heat in it 1 tbsp. of oil.
4. Cook in it the onion with garlic for 2 min. Stir in the cumin and cook them for 1 min.
5. Stir in the harissa with tomatoes, a pinch of salt and pepper. Cook them while stirring until they become thick.
6. Add the prawns and cook them for 4 min while stirring.
7. Transfer the couscous to a serving plate. Top it with the prawn sauce and garnish it with coriander then serve it.
8. Enjoy.

Couscous
Tunis

🥣 Prep Time: 10 mins
🕐 Total Time: 40 mins

Servings per Recipe: 4
Calories	791.2
Fat	34.9 g
Cholesterol	15.2 mg
Sodium	418.0 mg
Carbohydrates	109.1 g
Protein	18.0 g

Ingredients

1/2 lb. couscous
1 1/4 C. hot water
2 tbsp. butter, melted
12 dates, stoned and chopped
12 almonds, whole
1 1/2 C. mixed nuts, finely chopped
2 tbsp. raisins, currants or 2 tbsp. sultanas

1/2 C. sugar
1 orange, juice of
1 tbsp. powdered sugar
1 tsp. ground cinnamon

Directions

1. Combine the hot water with couscous in a mixing bowl. Stir them well.
2. Put on the lid and let it sit for 10 to 12 min.
3. Get a mixing bowl: Stir in it the dates with mixed nuts, dried fruit, sugar and orange juice.
4. Transfer the couscous to a steamer and steam it for 10 min.
5. Transfer it back to the bowl. Add to it the butter and mix them well. Steam it for an extra 8 min.
6. Transfer the couscous to serving plates. Pour over them the fruity mixture.
7. Garnish them with almonds, powdered sugar and cinnamon then serve them.
8. Enjoy.

APPLE AND BEETS
COUSCOUS

Prep Time: 10 mins
Total Time: 45 mins

Servings per Recipe: 4
Calories	92.4
Fat	0.3 g
Cholesterol	0.0 mg
Sodium	75.4 mg
Carbohydrates	19.1 g
Protein	2.8 g

Ingredients
1/8 tsp. extra virgin olive oil
1/8 C. red onion, diced
1/2 C. couscous, grande
1/4 C. unsweetened apple juice
3/4 C. beet juice
1/4 tsp. cinnamon

1/8 tsp. sea salt
1 dash white pepper

Directions
1. Place a large saucepan over high heat. Heat in it the oil.
2. Cook in it the onion for 2 min. Stir in the couscous, apple juice, beet juice, and seasonings.
3. Cook them until they start boiling. Lower the heat and put on the lid.
4. Let them cook until the couscous absorbs all the liquid. Serve it warm.
5. Enjoy.

Lebanese
Parsley Salad (Tabbouleh)

🥣 Prep Time: 20 mins
🕐 Total Time: 25 mins

Servings per Recipe: 6
Calories	368.7
Fat	13.5 g
Cholesterol	0.0 mg
Sodium	181.6 mg
Carbohydrates	55.1 g
Protein	10.4 g

Ingredients

1 1/2 C. couscous
1 1/2 C. boiling water
1/3 C. extra virgin olive oil
1 tbsp. ground cumin
300 g chickpeas, rinsed & drained
3 C. flat leaf parsley, chopped
1 C. mint leaf, chopped

6 green onions, finely chopped
3 tomatoes, seeded & chopped
2 lemons, juiced
salt & pepper

Directions

1. Get a mixing bowl: Place in it the couscous and cover it with water.
2. Put on the lid and let it sit for 4 min. Stir it with a fork and place it aside.
3. Place a skillet over high heat. Heat in it 1 tbsp. of oil.
4. Cook in it the chickpeas with cumin for 4 to 5 min while stirring.
5. Add the mixture to the couscous with tomatoes, onion, mint, parsley, a pinch of salt and pepper.
6. Get a mixing bowl: Whisk in it the lemon juice with olive oil.
7. Add it to the couscous and mix them well. Serve it warm or chilled.
8. Enjoy.

SWEET
Apricot Couscous

Prep Time: 5 mins

Total Time: 20 mins

Servings per Recipe: 4
Calories	618.9
Fat	27.8 g
Cholesterol	58.6 mg
Sodium	174.3 mg
Carbohydrates	80.4 g
Protein	13.9 g

Ingredients

1/2 C. mixed pistachio nuts, toasted and roughly chopped
1/4 C. dried apricot, julienned
1 1/3 C. couscous
1/4 C. superfine sugar
3 tbsp. superfine sugar

6 tbsp. butter, softened
1/2 tsp. ground cinnamon
1 1/2 C. hot milk

Directions

1. Get a mixing bowl: Mix in it the chopped nuts with apricots.
2. Get a large mixing bowl: Stir in it the sugar with couscous and 1 C. of boiling water.
3. Stir in the butter with a pinch of salt until it melts.
4. Put on the lid and let it sit for 10 to 12 min. Mix it with a fork.
5. Add the apricot mixture and combine them well.
6. Garnish your couscous with some cinnamon then serve it with hot milk.
7. Enjoy.

Honey
Balsamic Couscous Bowls

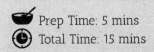 Prep Time: 5 mins
Total Time: 15 mins

Servings per Recipe: 6
Calories   93.0
Fat   2.9 g
Cholesterol   7.4 mg
Sodium   55.0 mg
Carbohydrates   14.9 g
Protein   2.5 g

Ingredients

1 1/2 C. water
1 C. whole wheat couscous
3 ripe plums, chopped
2 scallions, thinly sliced
2 oz. aged goat cheese, crumbled
1/4 C. chopped of fresh mint
3 tbsp. honey

3 1/2 tbsp. balsamic vinegar
salt and pepper, to taste

Directions

1. Prepare the couscous by following the instructions on the package.
2. Mix it with a fork the let it cool down for a while.
3. Stir in the plums, scallions, cheese, and mint.
4. Get a mixing bowl: Mix in it the vinegar with honey, a pinch of salt and pepper.
5. Add it to the couscous and mix them well. Serve your couscous warm or chilled.
6. Enjoy.

BABY
COUSCOUS

Prep Time: 10 mins
Total Time: 20 mins

Servings per Recipe: 2
Calories   406.1
Fat   7.7 g
Cholesterol   0.0 mg
Sodium   18.5 mg
Carbohydrates   70.4 g
Protein   13.8 g

Ingredients
1/2 C. chopped shallot
2 garlic cloves, minced
1 tbsp. oil
1/2 tsp. ground cumin
1 C. vegetable stock
1 C. frozen baby sweet peas

1/2 C. diced tomato, seeds removed
3/4 C. couscous, uncooked
salt and pepper, to taste

Directions
1. Place a pot over high heat. Heat in it the oil.
2. Cook in it the shallot with garlic for 2 min. add the cumin and cook them for 2 min.
3. Stir in the tomatoes with peas and broth. Cook them until they start simmering.
4. Add the couscous and put on the lid. Turn off the heat and let them sit for 6 min.
5. Mix it with a fork then serve it warm.
6. Enjoy.

Indian
Pilau
(Pilaf)

 Prep Time: 10 mins
🕐 Total Time: 45 mins

Servings per Recipe: 4
Calories   216.9
Fat   3.5 g
Cholesterol   7.8 mg
Sodium   529.3 mg
Carbohydrates   39.3 g
Protein   6.4 g

Ingredients
1 onion, chopped
2 carrots, sliced
2 chicken bouillon cubes
salt
pepper

1 C. couscous
1 tbsp. butter

Directions
1. Place a pot over high heat. Stir in it the chicken bouillon cubes in 2 ½ C. water.
2. Heat them until they start boiling. Stir in the onion with carrots.
3. Put on the lid and lower the heat. Bring them to a rolling boil for 16 min.
4. Stir in the couscous with a pinch of salt and pepper. Cook them while stirring for 1 to 2 min.
5. Stir in the butter and cook them for an extra minute.
6. Put on the lid and let it sit for 12 min. Serve it warm.
7. Enjoy.

COUSCOUS
Mornings

Prep Time: 10 mins
Total Time: 25 mins

Servings per Recipe: 2
Calories   446.3
Fat   10.0 g
Cholesterol   6.0 mg
Sodium   321.6 mg
Carbohydrates   71.6 g
Protein   18.6 g

Ingredients

1/2 C. instant couscous
1/2 C. nonfat dry milk powder
1/4 C. dried cherries
1/4 C. walnuts, finely chopped
3 tbsp. light brown sugar
1/2 tsp. ground cinnamon

1/8 tsp. salt
1 1/4 C. water

Directions

1. Get a mixing bowl: Mix in it the couscous with milk powder, cherries, walnuts, brown sugar, cinnamon, and salt.
2. Place a large saucepan over high heat. Heat in it the water until it starts boiling.
3. Add the couscous mixture and put on the lid. Turn off the heat and let it sit for 10 to 12 min.
4. Mix it with a fork then serve it.
5. Enjoy.

Orange Mango Mint Couscous Salad

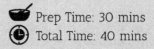 Prep Time: 30 mins

Total Time: 40 mins

Servings per Recipe: 4

Calories	249.8
Fat	7.3 g
Cholesterol	0.0 mg
Sodium	297.2 mg
Carbohydrates	41.9 g
Protein	5.2 g

Ingredients

1/2 C. orange juice
1/3 C. water
1/2 tsp. salt, divided
3/4 C. whole wheat couscous
1 C. blueberries
1 C. mango, cut into cubes
1/3 C. red onion, chopped

2 tbsp. mint, chopped
2 tbsp. lemon juice
2 tbsp. olive oil
1/8 tsp. pepper

Directions

1. Place a pot over high heat. Combine in it the water with orange juice and 1/4 tsp. of salt.
2. Heat them until they start boiling. Add the couscous and put on the lid.
3. Turn off the heat and let them sit for 6 min.
4. Pour the couscous into a large serving bowl. Stir it with a fork then let sit for 10 to 12 min to lose heat.
5. Get a mixing bowl: Stir in it the blueberries with mango, onion, mint, lemon juice, olive oil, pepper, and salt.
6. Add it to the couscous and stir them well. Serve it right away.
7. Enjoy.

ZUCCHINI
Seafood Salad

Prep Time: 18 mins
Total Time: 28 mins

Servings per Recipe: 4
Calories	478.7
Fat	13.2 g
Cholesterol	52.1 mg
Sodium	563.8 mg
Carbohydrates	53.0 g
Protein	34.8 g

Ingredients

1 1/3 C. couscous
2 1/3 C. chicken broth
1 small garlic clove, minced
3 medium carrots, peeled and shredded
1/2 lb. tomatoes, chopped
1 small zucchini, thinly sliced
1/4 C. fresh cilantro, chopped
1 tbsp. fresh mint leaves, make into tight
bundle and slice very finely

2 tbsp. olive oil
1 lb. salmon
salt and pepper, to taste
lemon wedge

Directions

1. Place a pot over high heat. Heat in it the broth until it starts boiling.
2. Stir in the couscous and turn off the heat. Put on the lid and let it sit for 12 min.
3. Stir in the garlic with carrot, tomatoes, zucchini, cilantro, mint, olive oil, a pinch of salt and pepper.
4. Before you do anything else, preheat the grill and grease it.
5. Coat the salmon with a cooking spray or some oil. Season it with a pinch of salt and pepper.
6. Grill it for 5 to 6 min on each side. Serve it warm with the couscous salad.
7. Enjoy.

Vegetarian
Couscous Platter

🥣 Prep Time: 5 mins
🕐 Total Time: 20 mins

Servings per Recipe: 6
Calories   280.9
Fat   1.8 g
Cholesterol   3.0 mg
Sodium   162.8 mg
Carbohydrates   53.8 g
Protein   11.1 g

Ingredients

2 1/2 C. chicken stock
1/2 tsp. ground cumin
1/4 tsp. paprika
1/4 tsp. ground black pepper
1/4 tsp. cinnamon
1/2 tsp. turmeric
1/2 C. chopped red onion
1/4 C. diced carrot
1/2 C. diced turnip

1/2 C. diced red pepper
1/2 C. diced zucchini
2 C. couscous
1/2 C. fresh peas
salt
3 tbsp. chopped fresh coriander

Directions

1. Place a large saucepan over medium heat. Heat in it the broth until it starts boiling.
2. Stir in the cumin, paprika, black pepper, cinnamon, and turmeric. Cook them for 2 to 3 min.
3. Stir in the onion, carrots, turnips, red pepper, peas and zucchini. Cook them for 6 min until they become tender.
4. Increase the heat to high then cook them until they start boiling.
5. Add the couscous and put on the lid. Let them sit for 6 min.
6. Stir the couscous salad with a fork then season it with a pinch of salt and pepper.
7. Garnish it with coriander then serve it.
8. Enjoy.

MEDITERRANEAN
Wedding Cake

Prep Time: 20 mins
Total Time: 1 hr 30 mins

Servings per Recipe: 10
Calories	296.8
Fat	6.8 g
Cholesterol	86.9 mg
Sodium	150.6 mg
Carbohydrates	55.1 g
Protein	5.5 g

Ingredients

For The Cake
1 1/2 C. water
1 1/2 C. pitted and coarsely chopped
Medjool dates
1/4 C. melted unsalted butter,
lukewarm
1/2 tsp. baking soda
1 C. unbleached all-purpose flour sifted
1/2 C. uncooked medium couscous

1 1/2 tsp. baking powder
1/2 C. sugar
4 eggs
For The Icing
1 C. icing sugar
5 tsp. milk

Directions

1. To prepare the cake:
2. Place the oven rack in the middle. Preheat the oven to 350 F.
3. Grease a spring form pan with some butter then dust it with flour. Place it aside.
4. Place a pot over high heat. Stir in it the water with butter and dates.
5. Cook them until they start boiling. Lower the heat and bring them to a simmer while stirring.
6. Pour the mixture into a bowl an let it cool down for a while. Put on the lid and chill it in the fridge for 35 min.
7. Get a mixing bowl: Mix in it the baking powder with couscous and flour.
8. Get a mixing bowl: Whisk in it the sugar with eggs until they become pale for 10 to 12 min. Add the flour mixture gradually and stir it gently followed by the dates mix.
9. Pour the batter into the greased pan and bake it for 1 h 5 min.
10. Allow your cake to lose heat completely.
11. To prepare the icing:
12. Get a mixing bowl:
13. Mix in it the milk with sugar until they become smooth.
14. Coat the cake with the icing then serve it. Enjoy.

30-Minute Weeknight Couscous

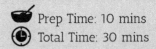
Prep Time: 10 mins
Total Time: 30 mins

Servings per Recipe: 1
Calories	427.4
Fat	7.0 g
Cholesterol	2.8 mg
Sodium	152.3 mg
Carbohydrates	77.5 g
Protein	12.0 g

Ingredients

2 C. couscous
2 C. boiling chicken stock
2 tbsp. olive oil
2 large brown onions, thinly sliced
2 garlic cloves, chopped
1/3 C. brown sugar
1/3 C. apple cider vinegar
2 tbsp. thyme, chopped
2/3 C. sultana (raisins)

Directions

1. Combine the stock with couscous in a large mixing bowl.
2. Cover it and let it sit for 6 min. Stir it with a fork then place it aside.
3. Place a large skillet over high heat. Heat in it the oil.
4. Cook in it the garlic with onion for 4 min. Add the sugar, vinegar, and thyme.
5. Cook them for 14 min while stirring. Add the mixture to the couscous with sultanas, a pinch of salt and pepper.
6. Mix them well. Serve your couscous warm or chilled.
7. Enjoy.

5-INGREDIENT
Zesty Couscous

Prep Time: 5 mins
Total Time: 10 mins

Servings per Recipe: 5
Calories	146.1
Fat	0.6 g
Cholesterol	1.0 mg
Sodium	55.3 mg
Carbohydrates	29.1 g
Protein	5.3 g

Ingredients
2 limes, zest of, grated
2 tbsp. coriander, chopped
1 C. couscous
3/4 C. chicken stock

1/4 C. lime juice

Directions
1. Place a large saucepan over high heat. Stir in it the stock with lime juice.
2. Bring them to a boil. Stir in the couscous and put on the lid. Let it sit for 6 min.
3. Add the coriander with lime zest and mix them well. Serve it warm or chilled.
4. Enjoy.

Hot
Broccoli Couscous

Prep Time: 5 mins
Total Time: 20 mins

Servings per Recipe: 2	
Calories	662.5
Fat	29.4 g
Cholesterol	0.0 mg
Sodium	608.9 mg
Carbohydrates	82.7 g
Protein	18.8 g

Ingredients

2 large tomatoes, cored and quartered
4 tbsp. olive oil
10 broccoli florets
60 g green beans, trimmed
175 g couscous
1/2 tsp. cinnamon
1/2 tsp. cumin
1/2 tsp. ground coriander

1/2 tsp. chili powder
300 ml hot chicken stock
1/2 lemon, juice of
200 g halloumi cheese, 4 to 6 slices, or feta
salt and pepper, to taste

Directions

1. Before you do anything, preheat the oven to 350 F.
2. Place the tomatoes on a baking sheet. Coat them with olive oil.
3. Sprinkle over them some salt and pepper. Bake them for 12 to 16 min.
4. Combine the beans with broccoli in a steamer. Cook them for 6 to 7 min.
5. Get a mixing bowl: Stir in it the couscous with cinnamon, cumin, coriander, chili powder, a pinch of salt and pepper.
6. Add the boiling stock and stir them well. put on the lid and let it sit for 6 min.
7. Once the time is up, add the broccoli with beans, and lemon juice. Mix them well.
8. Transfer the mixture to a serving plate. Garnish it with tomatoes and halloumi cheese.
9. Enjoy.
10. Place a skillet over high heat. Cook in it the halloumi cheese for 1 to 2 min on each side. Place it aside.

FULL COUSCOUS
Lunch Box Salad

Prep Time: 10 mins
Total Time: 20 mins

Servings per Recipe: 6
Calories	252.6
Fat	14.7 g
Cholesterol	0.0 mg
Sodium	1085.8 mg
Carbohydrates	26.9 g
Protein	4.5 g

Ingredients

1 C. couscous
2 garlic cloves, mashed
1 tsp. salt
2 tbsp. lemon juice, freshly squeezed
1 tsp. Dijon mustard
2 tsp. white balsamic vinegar
3 tbsp. extra virgin olive oil
fresh ground black pepper

1 1/3 C. black olives
1 1/3 C. green olives
1/4 C. red onion, finely diced
1/2 C. fresh cilantro, minced or 1/2 C. flat leaf parsley
2 - 3 tbsp. of fresh mint, minced
1/4 C. parmesan cheese

Directions

1. Place a pot over high heat. Heat in it 2 1/2 C. of water until they start boiling.

2. Stir in the salt with couscous. Put on the lid and lower the heat.

3. Let them cook for 6 min. Turn off the heat and let it sit for 8 min.

4. Once the time is up, drain it and place it aside to cool down.

5. Get a food processor: Combine in it the garlic with salt, lemon juice, mustard, vinegar, olive oil, and pepper.

6. Blend them smooth. Add it to the couscous with olives, red onion, mint, and cilantro.

7. Mix them well. Chill your couscous in the fridge until ready to serve.

8. Enjoy.

Glazed
Greek Couscous

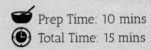 Prep Time: 10 mins
Total Time: 15 mins

Servings per Recipe: 6
Calories   167.0
Fat   2.9 g
Cholesterol   1.4 mg
Sodium   229.8 mg
Carbohydrates   29.5 g
Protein   5.8 g

Ingredients

1 1/4 C. water
1 C. uncooked couscous
1/2 C. low-fat buttermilk
1/4 C. plain low-fat yogurt
2 tbsp. chopped fresh dill
2 tbsp. white vinegar
1 tbsp. olive oil
1/2 tsp. salt

1/4 tsp. black pepper
1 C. chopped red bell pepper
1/4 C. thinly sliced green onion
2 cucumbers, peeled, quartered lengthwise, and sliced(about 3/4 lb.)

Directions

1. Place a pot over high heat. Heat in it the water until it starts boiling.
2. Stir in the couscous and turn off the heat. Put on the lid and let it sit for 6 min.
3. Stir it with a fork then place it aside to lose heat completely.
4. Get a mixing bowl: Whisk in it the buttermilk with yogurt, dill, vinegar, olive oil, salt, and pepper.
5. Stir in the couscous, bell pepper, onions, and cucumbers.
6. Chill your salad in the fridge for at least 15 min then serve it.
7. Enjoy.

DESSERT
COUSCOUS

Prep Time: 20 mins
Total Time: 30 mins

Servings per Recipe: 4
Calories	611.6
Fat	23.5 g
Cholesterol	36.6 mg
Sodium	139.7 mg
Carbohydrates	88.4 g
Protein	14.9 g

Ingredients
1 C. whole milk
1/2 C. blanched almond, very finely chopped
4 tbsp. butter
1 1/2 C. couscous
salt
1/4 C. raisins

1/4 C. dried apricot, chopped
1/4 C. dates, chopped
1/4 C. sugar
1/2 tsp. ground cinnamon

Directions
1. Place a heavy saucepan over high heat. Heat in it the milk with almonds until it starts boiling.
2. Turn off the heat and put on the lid. Place it aside to cool down.
3. Place a pot over medium heat. Heat in it the butter until it melts.
4. Stir in the couscous and cook them for 60 min. Stir in 2 1/4 C. of water and a pinch of salt.
5. Cook them until they start boiling. Lower the heat and put on the lid.
6. Let them cook for 10 to 14 min.
7. Get a mixing bowl: Combine in it the raisins, apricots, and dates.
8. Cover them with warm water and let them sit for a while until they become soft.
9. Transfer the couscous to a serving bowl. Mix into it the fruits after draining along with the remaining butter.
10. Add the sugar with cinnamon. Mix them well.
11. Strain the almond milk then drizzle all over the couscous.
12. Enjoy.

How to Make
Israeli Couscous

Prep Time: 10 mins
Total Time: 20 mins

Servings per Recipe: 6
Calories   221.0
Fat   4.9 g
Cholesterol   0.0 mg
Sodium   21.0 mg
Carbohydrates   37.4 g
Protein   6.6 g

Ingredients

1 1/2 C. Israeli couscous
3 C. cauliflower florets
1/4 tsp. cinnamon
1 tsp. coriander
1 shallot, sliced
2 tbsp. olive oil, divided
1/3 C. dried cranberries

salt and pepper
apple cider vinegar, splash
chopped parsley

Directions

1. Prepare the couscous by following the instructions on the package.
2. Drain it, run it under cold water and drain it again.
3. Transfer it to a mixing bowl. Add 1 tbsp. of olive oil and a pinch of salt. Mix them well.
4. Place a large skillet over high heat. Heat in it the rest of the oil.
5. Stir in it 3 C. of cauliflower with the sliced shallot. Cook them for 10 to 12 min while stirring.
6. Stir in the cinnamon with coriander, a pinch of salt and pepper. Cook them for 1 min.
7. Stir in 1/3 C. dried cranberries. Cook them for 2 to 3 min while stirring often.
8. Add the mixture to couscous with a splash of apple cider vinegar, and salt and pepper.
9. Serve it warm.
10. Enjoy.

LEILA'S
Award Winning Couscous

Prep Time: 20 mins
Total Time: 1 hr 50 mins

Servings per Recipe: 4
Calories	474.4
Fat	8.8 g
Cholesterol	74.8 mg
Sodium	884.9 mg
Carbohydrates	70.1 g
Protein	32.4 g

Ingredients
1 tbsp. vegetable oil
1 lb. boneless beef roast, in 3/4 inch chunks
1/2 tsp. salt
1/8 tsp. pepper
2 1/4 C. beef stock
1 1/2 tsp. cinnamon
8 oz. white pearl onions, peeled

8 oz. butternut squash, in 1/2 inch cubes
3 tbsp. vinegar
1 tbsp. honey
1 C. pitted prune
3/4 C. couscous

Directions
1. Place a pot over high heat. Heat in it the oil.
2. Stir in it the beef chunks with a pinch of salt and pepper. Cook them for 7 min while stirring.
3. Stir in the cinnamon with stock. Cook them until they start boiling.
4. Add the onions, squash or sweet potato, vinegar, and honey.
5. Cook them until they start boiling. Lower the heat and put on the lid.
6. Let them cook for 32 min.
7. Stir in the prunes and put on the lid. Bring them to a rolling boil for 3 min.
8. Prepare the couscous by following the instructions on the package.
9. Transfer it to serving plates. Top it with the meat stew then serve it.
10. Enjoy.

Almond and Date
COUSCOUS

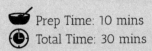
Prep Time: 10 mins
Total Time: 30 mins

Servings per Recipe: 4
Calories	335.3
Fat	6.7 g
Cholesterol	0.0 mg
Sodium	8.3 mg
Carbohydrates	63.0 g
Protein	8.4 g

Ingredients
1 C. couscous
1 tbsp. tahini
1/2 tsp. cinnamon
1/4 tsp. ground cardamom
6 large pitted dates, chopped into pieces

1/3 C. slivered almonds
4 tbsp. honey

Directions
1. Place a pot over high heat. Stir in it 2 C. of water with a pinch of salt.
2. Heat it until it starts boiling. Stir in the tahini, cardamom, and cinnamon.
3. Lower the heat and stir in the couscous. Put on the lid and let it cook for 16 to 22 min.
4. Stir it with a fork, drain it transfer it to a serving bowl.
5. Add to it the almonds, chopped dates, and creamed honey. Stir them to coat.
6. Garnish it with cinnamon then serve it with some hot tea.
7. Enjoy.

CASABLANCA
Café Pudding

Prep Time: 1 hr
Total Time: 1 hr 10 mins

Servings per Recipe: 6	
Calories	223.5
Fat	2.2 g
Cholesterol	7.8 mg
Sodium	31.8 mg
Carbohydrates	42.5 g
Protein	7.5 g

Ingredients
1/2 C. milk
3 tbsp. sugar
1/4 C. dried cherries
1 vanilla bean
1 1/2 C. couscous, steamed

8 oz. vanilla yogurt
1/4 tsp. ground cinnamon

Directions
1. Place a pot over medium heat. Stir in it the milk, sugar, and cherries.
2. Heat them until they start simmering. Turn off the heat and put on the lid.
3. Let them sit for 10 to 12 min. Add the vanilla seeds and stir them well.
4. Place the couscous in a mixing bowl. Add to it the hot milk mixture with yogurt and stir them well.
5. Spoon the pudding into serving bowls. Chill them in the fridge for at least 60 min before serving.
6. Enjoy.

Nutty Mintye
Couscous Sampler

Prep Time: 15 mins
Total Time: 25 mins

Servings per Recipe: 4
Calories   393.8
Fat   11.5 g
Cholesterol   0.0 mg
Sodium   343.2 mg
Carbohydrates   59.0 g
Protein   13.6 g

Ingredients

1/4 C. pistachios, shelled
2 1/2 C. low sodium chicken broth
1/2 tsp. salt
1 (10 oz.) boxes couscous
1/8-1/4 C. fresh mint leaves, chopped
2 tbsp. olive oil

1 tsp. fresh lemon juice
ground pepper, to taste

Directions

1. Before you do anything, preheat the oven to 350 F.
2. Place the pistachios in a baking sheet. Toast them in the oven for 9 min.
3. Place them aside to cool down then coarsely chop them.
4. Place a pot over high heat. Heat in it the broth with a pinch of salt until they start boiling.
5. Stir in the couscous and put on the lid. Let them sit for 6 min.
6. Stir it with a fork then transfer it to a serving bowl.
7. Add to it the pistachios, mint, oil, lemon juice, a pinch of salt and pepper.
8. Serve it with extra toppings of your choice.
9. Enjoy.

TROPICAL
COUSCOUS

Prep Time: 15 mins
Total Time: 25 mins

Servings per Recipe: 8
Calories	300.9
Fat	9.5 g
Cholesterol	0.0 mg
Sodium	73.9 mg
Carbohydrates	48.9 g
Protein	6.6 g

Ingredients

1 (11 oz.) cans mandarin oranges, liquid reserved
2 1/4 C. orange juice
1 1/2 tsp. ground cumin
1 (10 oz.) boxes couscous
3 tbsp. olive oil
1 tbsp. reduced sodium soy sauce
3 tbsp. lime juice, fresh
1/4 C. cilantro, freshly chopped
2 tbsp. basil, freshly chopped

3 tbsp. green onions, freshly chopped
1 1/2 tsp. ginger, freshly chopped
1 (15 1/4 oz.) cans pineapple tidbits, drained
1/3 C. pine nuts, toasted

Directions

1. Pour the mandarin orange liquid in a measuring C. Add to it enough orange juice to make 2 1/4 C. of it.
2. Pour it into a large saucepan. Add the cumin and heat it until it starts boiling.
3. Turn off the heat and stir in the couscous. Put on the lid and let it sit for 6 min.
4. Fluff it with a fork and transfer it to a serving bowl. Let it cool down completely.
5. Get a mixing bowl: Whisk in it the oil, soy sauce, and lime juice.
6. Add it to the couscous with mandarin oranges, cilantro, basil, green onions, ginger, and pineapple.
7. Mix them well. Garnish it with pine nuts then serve it.
8. Enjoy.

Friendship
COUSCOUS

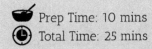 Prep Time: 10 mins

Total Time: 25 mins

Servings per Recipe: 6
Calories   306.3
Fat   9.6 g
Cholesterol   11.9 mg
Sodium   130.0 mg
Carbohydrates   45.9 g
Protein   9.2 g

Ingredients
1 zucchini, finely diced
1 tomatoes, finely diced
1 C. sweet peas
4 garlic cloves, finely chopped
2 tbsp. extra virgin olive oil
1 1/2 C. chicken stock
1 1/2 C. couscous

1 granny smith apple, finely diced
2 tbsp. of fresh mint, chopped
2 tbsp. butter
salt and pepper

Directions
1. Place a pot over high heat. Heat in it the oil.
2. Cook in it the zucchini with tomatoes, peas, and garlic for 3 min.
3. Stir in the stock and cook them until they start boiling.
4. Stir in the couscous with a pinch of salt and pepper.
5. Put on the lid and turn off the heat. Let it sit for 6 min.
6. stir it with a fork. Add the apples with mint and butter. Mix them well.
7. Serve your couscous warm or chilled.
8. Enjoy.

LIGHT
Couscous Snack

Prep Time: 20 mins
Total Time: 45 mins

Servings per Recipe: 4
Calories	494.6
Fat	24.2 g
Cholesterol	0.0 mg
Sodium	527.9 mg
Carbohydrates	53.0 g
Protein	19.1 g

Ingredients

2 tbsp. Crisco pure canola oil
1/2 C. onion, chopped
1/4 C. green bell pepper, diced
2-3 garlic clove, minced
1 1/2 C. chicken broth
1/2 C. crunchy peanut butter

1/2 tsp. ground cumin
salt and pepper
1 (10 oz.) packages frozen peas
1 C. couscous

Directions

1. Place a pot over medium heat. Heat in it the canola oil.
2. Cook in it the onions, bell pepper, and garlic for 4 min.
3. Stir in the broth and cook them until they start boiling.
4. Get a mixing bowl: Mix in it the peanut butter with cumin, a pinch of salt and pepper.
5. Stir it into the pot with peas. Cook them until they start boiling again.
6. Add the couscous and bring them to another boil while stirring often.
7. Turn off the heat and put on the lid. Let it sit for 6 min.
8. Stir it with a fork then serve it.
9. Enjoy.

North African
Seafood Couscous

🥣 Prep Time: 10 mins
🕐 Total Time: 15 mins

Servings per Recipe: 1
Calories	431.9
Fat	8.6 g
Cholesterol	17.1 mg
Sodium	371.0 mg
Carbohydrates	52.0 g
Protein	36.9 g

Ingredients

1/4 C. couscous
1 tsp. Moroccan seasoning i.e. ras el
hanout, see appendix
1/4 C. boiling water
1 tbsp. lemon juice
Oz. tuna in brine, drained and flaked
2 green shallots, ends trimmed and finely
chopped

1 tomatoes, coarsely chopped
1/4 Lebanese cucumber, finely chopped
1/4 green capsicum, deseeded, finely chopped
1 tbsp. shredded of fresh mint
2 lettuce leaves

Directions

1. Get a mixing bowl: Stir in it the couscous with the Moroccan seasoning.
2. Stir into it the boiling water and put on the lid. Let sit for 6 min.
3. Stir it with a fork. Mix in the lemon juice, tuna, shallot, tomato, cucumber, capsicum, and mint.
4. Allow your couscous salad to sit for few minutes then serve it with the lettuce leaves.
5. Enjoy.

LOS ANGELES
Meets Morocco Tacos

Prep Time: 5 mins
Total Time: 20 mins

Servings per Recipe: 5
Calories	315.0
Fat	12.4 g
Cholesterol	15.8 mg
Sodium	534.6 mg
Carbohydrates	38.7 g
Protein	13.0 g

Ingredients

1 (14 1/2 oz.) cans Mexican-style
stewed tomatoes
1 C. water
1/4 C. chopped onion
5 tsp. taco seasoning mix
2/3 C. couscous
8 oz. firm tofu, drained and finely
chopped

10 taco shells, warmed
1 1/2 C. shredded lettuce
2/3 C. shredded cheddar cheese (about
3 oz.)
salsa

Directions

1. Place a pot over high heat. Stir in it the stewed tomatoes, water, onion, and taco seasoning mix.
2. Cook them until they start boiling. Add the tofu with couscous.
3. Put on the lid and turn off the heat. Let it sit for 6 min.
4. Transfer the couscous mixture into the taco shells.
5. Top them with lettuce, cheese, and salsa.
6. Enjoy.

Parsley and Cheese
COUSCOUS

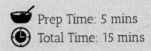

Prep Time: 5 mins
Total Time: 15 mins

Servings per Recipe: 4
Calories	92.4
Fat	5.2 g
Cholesterol	0.0 mg
Sodium	6.2 mg
Carbohydrates	9.8 g
Protein	1.7 g

Ingredients
1 C. cooked couscous
6 oz. halloumi cheese, or feta
1 tbsp. lemon zest, finely grated
1/2 C. flat leaf parsley
1 1/2 tbsp. vegetable oil

Directions
1. Get a food processor: Combine in it the couscous, halloumi, lemon zest, and parsley.
2. Pulse them several times until they become finely chopped.
3. Form every 1/4 C. of the mixture into a pattie.
4. Place a large skillet over medium heat. Heat in it the oil.
5. Fry the couscous patties for 3 min on each side. Serve them warm with toppings of your choice.
6. Enjoy.

ARABIAN
Couscous Bowl

🍲 Prep Time: 7 mins
🕐 Total Time: 7 mins

Servings per Recipe: 1
Calories	786.0
Fat	18.6 g
Cholesterol	2.5 mg
Sodium	176.4 mg
Carbohydrates	134.7 g
Protein	22.2 g

Ingredients

3 - 4 large carrots, julienne
2 dates, chopped
3 tbsp. walnuts, chopped
3/4 C. couscous
3/4 C. boiling water
1/4 tsp. butter

1/2 tsp. olive oil
salt and pepper, to taste

Directions

1. Bring a salted pot of water to a boil. Cook in it the carrots for 6 min until they become soft.
2. Drain them and place them aside.
3. Prepare the couscous by following the instructions on the package.
4. Fluff it with a fork. Add the olive oil and mix them well.
5. Place a heavy pan over medium heat. Stir in it the carrots with butter.
6. Cook them for 3 to 5 min while stirring.
7. Transfer the couscous to a serving plate. Top it with the carrot mixture followed by dates and walnuts.
8. Adjust its seasoning then serve it.
9. Enjoy.

Garlic Chili
COUSCOUS

🥣 Prep Time: 5 mins
🕐 Total Time: 20 mins

Servings per Recipe: 6
Calories	377.4
Fat	13.1 g
Cholesterol	14.8 mg
Sodium	214.6 mg
Carbohydrates	49.1 g
Protein	18.2 g

Ingredients

1 1/2 C. couscous
2 tbsp. olive oil
1 green chili pepper, seeded and minced
1 tsp. ground cumin
1 tsp. ground coriander
2 minced garlic cloves
1 1/2 C. frozen shelled edamame
3 C. cherry tomatoes halved
1 C. of fresh mint, chopped

1 bunch scallion, sliced
1 tbsp. fresh lemon juice
2/3 C. crumbled feta cheese
black olives, if desired(kalamata)
salt and pepper, to taste

Directions

1. Get a mixing bowl: Stir in it the couscous, ½ tbsp. olive oil, minced chili, cumin, coriander, and garlic and edamame.
2. Stir in 2 C. of boiling water. Put on the lid and let them sit for 6 min.
3. Get a mixing bowl: Stir in it the tomatoes, mint or basil leaves, scallions, and lemon juice.
4. Add the couscous with the rest of the olive oil, feta cheese, a pinch of salt and pepper.
5. Toss them to coat then transfer them to a serving plate.
6. Garnish your salad with some black olives then serve it.
7. Enjoy.

AZTEC
Couscous

Prep Time: 2 mins
Total Time: 12 mins

Servings per Recipe: 4
Calories   335.3
Fat   2.2 g
Cholesterol   0.0 mg
Sodium   686.2 mg
Carbohydrates   62.9 g
Protein   15.9 g

Ingredients

1 C. couscous
1 1/2 C. chicken broth
1 C. water
1 (19 oz.) cans kidney beans, drained
1 taco seasoning

1 red pepper, chopped
1 C. corn

Directions

1. Place a large saucepan over low heat.
2. Stir in it all the ingredients. Let them cook until the couscous absorbs all the liquid.
3. Serve it warm.
4. Enjoy.

Peppery
Potato Couscous

Prep Time: 15 mins
Total Time: 1 hr 35 mins

Servings per Recipe: 4
Calories	361.6
Fat	2.5 g
Cholesterol	0.0 mg
Sodium	681.7 mg
Carbohydrates	75.6 g
Protein	13.3 g

Ingredients

1 large onion, chopped
1/2 tsp. turmeric
1/4 tsp. cayenne
1/2 C. vegetable stock
1/2 tbsp. cinnamon
1 1/2 tsp. black pepper
1/2 tsp. salt
5 tbsp. tomato puree
3 - 4 whole cloves

3 medium zucchini, chopped
4 small yellow squash, chopped
3/4 large carrot, chopped
4 medium yellow potatoes, skins on, chopped
1 red bell pepper, chopped
1 (15 oz.) cans garbanzo beans

Directions

1. Place a pot over medium heat. Grease it with a cooking spray.
2. Stir in the onion and cook it for 3 min. Stir in the seasonings and cook them for 1 min.
3. Stir in the tomato paste and cook them for 1 to 2 min while stirring.
4. Stir in the veggies and cover them with water.
5. Cook them until they start boiling. Lower the heat and put on the lid.
6. Let them cook for 60 min. stir in the chickpeas and cook them for 6 min.
7. Get a mixing bowl: Place in it the couscous and cover it with boiling water.
8. Put on the lid and let it sit for 6 min. Stir it with a fork and season it with a pinch of salt and pepper.
9. Transfer the couscous to a serving plate. Spoon over it the veggies stew then serve it.
10. Enjoy.

HOMEMADE
Garam Masala Spice Mix

Prep Time: 5 mins
Total Time: 5 mins

Servings per Recipe: 8
Calories   24 kcal
Fat   0.7 g
Carbohydrates   4.1g
Protein   0.8 g
Cholesterol   0 mg
Sodium   6 mg

Ingredients

1/4 C. black cumin seed
2 large bay leaves, crushed
2 tbsps green cardamom seeds
1/4 C. black peppercorns
1 1/2 tsps whole cloves
1 tbsp fennel seed

1 tsp chopped fresh mace
4 cinnamon sticks, broken
1 pinch ground nutmeg

Directions

1. Toast the following in a skillet for 11 mins: cinnamon sticks, cumin, mace, bay leaves. Fennel seed, cardamom, cloves, and peppercorns.

2. With your grinder or mortar and pestle process the spices into a fine powder and store in your favorite container.

North African
Spice Mix
(Ras El Hanout)

🥣 Prep Time: 10 mins
🕐 Total Time: 10 mins

Servings per Recipe: 1
Calories	19.1
Fat	0.6 g
Cholesterol	0.0 mg
Sodium	583.9 mg
Carbohydrates	3.8 g
Protein	0.4 g

Ingredients

2 tsp ground nutmeg
2 tsp ground coriander
2 tsp ground cumin
2 tsp ground ginger
2 tsp turmeric
2 tsp salt
2 tsp cinnamon
1 1/2 tsp sugar
1 1/2 tsp paprika

1 1/2 tsp ground black pepper
1 tsp cayenne pepper
1 tsp cardamom powder
1 tsp ground allspice
1/2 tsp ground cloves

Directions

1. In a bowl, add all the ingredients and mix well.
2. Transfer the mixture into a glass jar and seal tightly.
3. Store in a cool, dry place.

SMOKED
Chili Harissa

🍲 Prep Time: 25 mins
🕐 Total Time: 35 mins

Servings per Recipe: 1
Calories   1115.6
Fat   111.4g
Cholesterol   0.0mg
Sodium   1200.5mg
Carbohydrates   32.2g
Protein   7.2g

Ingredients

4 smoked chili peppers, seeded
8 dried hot red chili peppers
1 tbsp cumin seed
2 tsp coriander seeds
1 tsp caraway seed
8 garlic cloves

1/2 C. olive oil
1/2 tsp salt

Directions

1. Place the chili peppers in a bowl. Cover them with hot water. Let them sit for 25 min then drain them.
2. Place a pan over medium heat. Cook in it the cumin, coriander, and caraway seeds 2 min.
3. Get a food processor: Place in it the toasted seeds with chilies, garlic, olive oil, and salt.
4. Process them until they become smooth. Spoon the mixture into an airtight container.
5. Store it in the fridge for up to 60 days.
6. Enjoy.

How to Make
Harissa

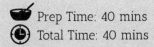

Prep Time: 40 mins
Total Time: 40 mins

Servings per Recipe: 8
Calories   73.4
Fat   2.7g
Cholesterol   0.0mg
Sodium   451.1mg
Carbohydrates   12.5g
Protein   2.0g

Ingredients
4.5 oz. dried hot red chili peppers, seeded
and stemmed
1/2 head garlic
1 1/2 tsps caraway seeds
1 1/2 tsps ground coriander
1 1/2 tsps salt

1 tsp water
1 - 3 tbsp olive oil

Directions
1. Get a bowl: Place in it the chili peppers and cover them with hot water. Let them sit for 30 min.
2. Strain them and transfer them to a food processor.
3. Add the garlic with the remaining ingredients. Blend them smooth.
4. Adjust the seasoning of your harissa then serve it.
5. Enjoy.

Printed in Great Britain
by Amazon

33800506R00057